THE
YOUNG ACTOR'S
HANDBOOK

THE APPLAUSE ACTING SERIES

THE YOUNG ACTOR'S HANDBOOK

JEREMY KRUSE

APPLAUSE
THEATRE & CINEMA BOOKS
AN IMPRINT OF HAL LEONARD LLC

Published in 2017 Applause Theatre & Cinema Books
An Imprint of Hal Leonard LLC
7777 West Bluemound Road
Milwaukee, WI 53213

Trade Book Division Editorial Offices
33 Plymouth St., Montclair, NJ 07042

Printed in the United States of America

Book design by Lynn Bergesen, UB Communications

Library of Congress Cataloging-in-Publication Data

Names: Kruse, Jeremy author.
Title: The young actor's handbook / Jeremy Kruse.
Description: Milwaukee, WI : Applause Theatre & Cinema Books, 2017.
Identifiers: LCCN 2016054162 | ISBN 9781495075421 (pbk.)
Subjects: LCSH: Monologues. | Acting. | Acting--Auditions.
Classification: LCC PN2080 .K78 2017 | DDC 808.82/45--dc23
LC record available at https://lccn.loc.gov/2016054162

www.applausebooks.com

CONTENTS

INTRODUCTION

Acting is the art of bringing a character to life. An actor does not figure out how to say the lines that are written for a character. An actor figures out why a character says the lines. If you are young or new to the art of acting, this book will help clarify what it means to be an actor. If you have experience or acting training, this book will serve as a refresher with new insights and inspiration. This book will be useful for teachers seeking student exercises, fresh insights or basic knowledge about the acting world. The acting exercises and short monologues in this book can be done at home, in a classroom, on a stage or on a film set. Any interior or exterior location will work.

The first section of this book includes the "Open-Ended Scene Exercise" and the "Hitting Your Mark and Continuity Exercise." These exercises are intended to get you, the actor, on your feet and introduce some very basic acting concepts.

The "Actor's Worksheet" and the "Advanced Actor's Worksheet" contained in this book will help guide you in making choices about your character, relationship, situation and other important elements.

The sections in this book, "Concepts," "Guidance," "Acting Techniques," "Film Acting," "Auditioning" and "The Business of Acting," will help you gain a deeper understanding of acting terms, concepts, what is means to be an actor and the art of acting.

The "Writing" section is designed for actors who have an interest in crafting their own stories. It gives a basic explanation of the elements that make up a story and contains writing exercises that will help a beginning writer generate story ideas for plays and screenplays.

The last section of the book contains original short monologues.

There are two ways to go about using this book:

1. You can read the whole book from beginning to end. From there, you can decide what you want to work on. You can move chronologically through the book or skip around.

2. You can start with the "Open-Ended Scene Exercise" and "Hitting Your Mark Exercise" in order to get warmed up. From there, you can read "Concepts," "Guidance," "Acting Techniques" and "Film Acting." Perhaps you will want to go back to the first exercise and practice what you've learned and then proceed with the rest of the chapters in the book.

CHAPTER 1

OPEN-ENDED SCENE EXERCISE

The open-ended scenes are for two actors. The character names are Actor A and Actor B. The characters are not age- or gender-specific. However, it is best that you choose to make your character close to your own age. It is rare, in the professional acting world, that you will play someone who is significantly older or younger than you.

Stories are about people in heightened situations, life-and-death situations. Every scene in a play or screenplay is important. A scene is designed to move a story forward in a small or large way. If a scene is casual, conversational or a "day in the life," then it is either bad writing, bad acting or part of a piece of work considered "non-genre."

If a character does not start at point A and end at point B, the story is not a narrative. Most stories that are written and executed are about people in heightened situations. It is the actor's responsibility to make strong choices in order to fuel a scene so that the scene carries weight.

If your character wants something and it is not life-or-death, then it is a weak choice. Great writing has this principle built in. If Little Red Riding Hood doesn't figure out a way to get away from the Big Bad Wolf, she will die. In the novel *The Old Man and the Sea*, Santiago risks his life to catch a marlin. Michael Corleone, in the film *The Godfather*, risks his life to save his family. If Michael is not 100 percent dedicated to saving his family and willing to risk his life, the story will fall flat. This principle applies to novels, plays and screenplays of any genre and of any length. It is your job, your obligation, to make strong choices.

The following scenes are completely open to interpretation. Use your imagination. Draw upon past experiences, invent details or both in order to bring the relationship, situation and character to life.

Before working on a scene, the basic choices to make are:

1. "Where am I?"

2. "What is my relationship to the other person in the scene?"

3. "What is happening in the scene?"

Be specific about your choices. The more specific you can be, the better. For the location, avoid choosing "at school." Where at school? In the cafeteria? The locker area in the hallway? The principal's office?

For the relationship, if you choose "my brother," be specific about how you feel about your brother: "my older brother, whom I look up to and revere."

When deciding what's happening in the scene, again, be specific. "I am devastated because my brother saw me in the hallway at school and didn't say hi to me. He made eye contact, but did not acknowledge my existence."

The choices you can make for this exercise are infinite. You are only limited by your imagination. The point of this exercise is that it doesn't matter what the lines are. What matters is what is happening underneath the lines. Avoid deciding how to say the lines. Avoid choosing what words to stress. Focus on the choices you make and allowing those choices to feed the scene and your behavior.

Avoid telling the actor with whom you are working what to do. Never impose your own ideas on another actor. Never tell another actor how to play a scene. Make the basic choices for this exercise with your partner and then make choices for your own character. Let your partner make his own choices. Actors do not like to be told what to do by other actors. You are only responsible for your own choices. It is the teacher's or director's job to guide each actor toward strong choices. If you are working without a teacher or director, kindly ask your partner if you can make a suggestion about how the scene can be played and see if your partner has any ideas.

A few questions to ask yourself with regard to choices before and after performing a scene are:

1. "Have I made the strongest possible choice?"

2. "How can I make this scene more interesting for me and for the audience?"

The "Actor's Worksheet" and the "Advanced Actor's Worksheet" contained in this book will help guide you while doing the exercises and making choices.

Do not focus on how to say the lines. Do not focus on creating emotion. Focus on your choices.

OPEN-ENDED SCENE #1

Actor A: Hi. Nice to see you.

Actor B: Nice to see you.

Actor A: You look good.

Actor B: I feel good.

Actor A: I have to go.

Actor B: So do I.

OPEN-ENDED SCENE #2

Actor A: I feel great.

Actor B: I don't.

Actor A: That's too bad.

Actor B: I don't think you understand.

Actor A: I don't.

Actor B: I feel a little better now.

OPEN-ENDED SCENE #3

Actor A: This is what I expected.

Actor B: That's surprising.

Actor A: Really? I don't know why.

Actor B: It just is.

Actor A: I'd like to know why.

Actor B: Think about it.

Actor A: I knew it.

OPEN-ENDED SCENE #4

Actor A: I feel bad for you.

Actor B: It's OK.

Actor A: It's unfair.

Actor B: Maybe you can help.

Actor A: I can't.

Actor B: It's OK.

OPEN-ENDED SCENE #5

Actor A: Good for you.

Actor B: It's not a big deal.

Actor A: It is. You deserve it.

Actor B: I did work hard.

Actor A: I helped.

Actor B: Sort of.

Actor A: I feel sick.

Actor B: You usually do.

OPEN-ENDED SCENE #6

Actor A: I knew it.

Actor B: I did, too.

Actor A: Tell the truth.

Actor B: OK.

OPEN-ENDED SCENE EXERCISE DIRECTIONS

Now that you have made your own choices, apply the following directions to the open-ended scenes.

Direction 1

Actor A—You have been grounded. You defied your parents and have not apologized. You are in your room. Your sibling comes up to see you.

Actor B—Your sibling has been grounded. He/she defied your parents and has not apologized. He/she is in his/her room. You go to see him/her.

Location: Bedroom

Direction 2

Actor A—You are a soldier for a militant group that is trying to save the world. A virus has wiped out a majority of the population. Actor B knows where a vaccine is and is keeping the location of the vaccine a secret.

Actor B—A virus has wiped out a majority of the population. You know the secret location of the vaccine. You have been captured by a militant group. You fear that if you reveal your secret, this group will use it for evil purposes.

Location: Jail cell

Direction 3

Actor A—You have just won a dance competition and have been selected to be part of a supergroup. You have to move to Miami, Florida, in order to rehearse, and then you will go on a yearlong tour of the world. Your friend, Actor B, was in the dance competition and came in last place.

Actor B—You have just been in a dance competition. You came in last place. Your friend, Actor A, won the dance competition.

Location: Lobby of the hotel where the competition took place

There are many benefits to doing the open-ended scenes. One of the benefits is having the freedom to make choices using your instincts. You also are getting on your feet right away before diving into the deep explanations of acting concepts. After doing the exercises a number of times, you will start to get an idea of what roles are right for you. Instead of blindly looking for material on which to work, you will be able to search for the kind of characters that resonate with you.

Again, your focus while doing the open-ended scenes should be on your choices. Your choices determine what's happening underneath the lines. You should not focus on giving meaning to the words. Your choices fuel the behavior. The words simply convey information. The information is important. The words can be beautiful and powerful as in the case of Shakespeare. But, the actor's job is to create the inner life of the character.

You have made your own choices to fuel the open-ended scenes. You have taken direction for the scenes. Now, take one of the groups of choices you have made or Direction 1, 2 and 3 and use the dialogue below. Focus on your group of choices or Direction 1, 2 and 3. Do not try to give meaning or make sense out of the dialogue below.

OPEN-ENDED SCENE #7

Actor A: Grass grows.
Actor B: I saw a dog.
Actor A: Vacations are fun.
Actor B: Hunger is real.
Actor A: Clocks tell time.
Actor B: Coins and a wallet.

CHAPTER 2

HITTING YOUR MARK AND CONTINUITY EXERCISE

The next group of scenes is intended to help you practice hitting marks and dealing with props on stage or on camera. As with the open-ended scenes, make strong choices.

Before you say the first line, on a specific word, during a pause, or after the last line:

1. Move to a different part of the stage or room (hit a mark). A mark is sometimes designated by putting a piece of tape on the floor.

2. Pick up or put down a prop.

In a professional situation, a director will often ask you to move and/or pick up a prop on a certain line, on a specific word or during a particular moment. It is expected that you can execute whatever physical demand is requested while staying in character.

Dealing with props is one of your major responsibilities. In the film world, it is especially important. You must be able to handle objects, as directed, for multiple takes in order to maintain continuity. Continuity is important with regard to editing. An actor has to pick up a glass of water, for example, on the same line and in the same way for every take. The movement and your hand placement have to be the same so that the film editor can cut together different angles. If the movement is different in one or more takes, editing becomes very difficult. Directors and editors love actors who make editing easy. Directors, both stage and film, love actors who can quickly and easily make physical adjustments while taking acting direction.

In most situations, you are expected to say the lines exactly as written. However, you might be asked to improvise. In that case, you are expected to be spontaneous and use your intuition in order to bring something original to the scene. When improvising, there are no boundaries and you are free to play and explore.

Try executing the following scenes with very detailed movements and saying the words exactly as written. Try multiple variations while staying in character. Then try improvising; execute the scene letting spontaneity and your intuition guide you.

There is only one actor who speaks in these scenes. Try the scene with one or more actors and try it alone.

If you are working in front of a camera, try executing these scenes in a wide, medium and close-up shot.

SCENE #1

Actor: I lose everything. (*Pause.*) I make notes about where I put things and I lose the notes. (*Pause.*) I lose everything.

SCENE #2

Actor: Nothing ever works out. (*Pause.*) I try so hard. (*Pause.*) Things are changing.

SCENE #3

Actor: This is so typical. (*Pause.*) You told me not to do it. I should have listened to you. (*Pause.*) I'm glad I didn't.

SCENE #4

Actor: This is a good day. (*Pause.*) No, it's not. It's really not. (*Pause.*) But it could be.

SCENE #5

Actor: I love it. It's great. (*Pause.*) I still have my doubts, though. (*Pause.*) I hate it. It's terrible.

SCENE #6

Actor: I don't believe it. (*Pause.*) That's not what I said. (*Pause.*) This is very unlike me.

CHAPTER 3

ACTOR'S WORKSHEET

Where am I?

_____

_____

_____

To whom am I talking?

_____

_____

_____

How do I feel about that person or those people?

_____

_____

_____

What has happened just before the scene begins?

_____

_____

_____

What is happening in the scene?

_____

_____

_____

What is happening with me? (What am I experiencing?)

_____

_____

_____

What do I want? (What is my need? What is my objective?)

_____

_____

_____

_____

How do I change in the scene?

_____

_____

_____

What can I, the actor, use from my own life that is similar to this situation, relationship or what the character is experiencing? What details can I, the actor, invent that are similar to this situation, relationship or what the character is experiencing? (Do not write anything personal. Write a word or two that will help you remember what you can use. Do not discuss anything personal with anyone. For example, write, "hallway high school." Don't write, "I was walking down the hallway and Lou knocked my books out of my hands and I cried and everyone laughed.")

_____

_____

_____

_____

CHAPTER 4

ADVANCED ACTOR'S WORKSHEET

The questions below are just a handful of the possibilities you might investigate about your character. The number of questions that can be asked is endless. The amount of time you can spend on each question is endless. You can either write out your answers or say them out loud.

A human being could spend a tremendous amount of time talking about every aspect of his life. He could tell stories about the past, explain his beliefs and talk about his hopes and dreams for the future. You, as the character, should be able to do the same. The better you know the character, the more real your character will be.

Writers give us some, but not all of the information that we need about our characters. If I am playing Hamlet, Shakespeare has told me that I attend college. But nowhere in the text is it stated what I study. I must decide this.

Answer the following questions from the character's point of view. For example, in response to the question "What do you do for fun?" you answer, "I love reading. Before I have finished one book, I am picking out my next book. Sometimes I spend hours at the library. One time, when I was at the library . . ."

You can make up whatever you want. You can make fun and interesting choices and change them as you please until your final rehearsals or first performance.

Home Life

1. Do you live with one parent? Both parents? Grandparent? Family member?

2. What is your relationship with that person like?

3. Do you have any siblings?

4. What is your relationship like with your siblings?

Social Life

1. Do you have a lot of friends? Groups of friends? One best friend? Are you a loner?

2. What is your relationship like with your friends if you have friends?

3. Do you like people?

4. Do you like talking to people?

School

1. Do you like school?

2. Are you a good student?

3. Do you ever get into trouble at school?

Work

1. Do you have a job?

2. Do you have chores that you have to do at home?

3. How do you feel about your job or your chores?

Extracurricular Activities

1. What do you do for fun?

2. Do you play sports?

3. Do you have any hobbies?

Religious Views

1. What are your religious views?

2. Are they the same as the views of your family? Your peers?

3. Do you express your views?

Political Views

1. What are your political views?

2. Are they the same as the views of your family? Your peers?

3. Do you express your views?

People change over time. Our circumstances and the way we feel when we are seven years old are often different than when we are twelve years old. What has changed in your life? The way we look often affects us and the people around us. Have you ever been treated negatively or positively because of the way you look or dress?

CHAPTER 5

CONCEPTS

S ome of the information presented in the following section is complicated. It may be necessary to read it multiple times before full comprehension is achieved.

As an acting teacher and coach, I do not present some of this information to students under the age of twelve.

SUBTEXT

The words are the "tip of the iceberg." Your primary focus is creating the character's inner life, experiencing something on stage and achieving your character's objective. The written words are secondary.

On stage, as in life, we usually say one thing while feeling something else. I could receive terrible news and then, when someone asks me how I am doing, I respond, "I'm doing well." What I have just expressed verbally is not necessarily what I am feeling. This is called subtext. I may tell someone, "I want you to stay," but what I am really saying is, "Get out." Subtext is the concept that what we think, feel and want is not exactly what we express in words.

You cannot understand your character's subtext until you understand your character's inner life and your character's objective.

INNER LIFE

The inner life of the character is what your character is experiencing. The inner life of your character is your character's reality. When we think about the inner life of a character, we narrow it down to exactly what the character is thinking, feeling and experiencing. For example, your character's inner life may be, "I love winning chess games and I will do anything to win as long as I don't hurt anyone or myself. I wish I were a better chess player. I should have worked harder. I feel sad." Or your character's inner life may be, "I need to get out of here. I can't stand these people in my class. I feel angry. I feel claustrophobic and sick to my stomach. But I have to stay or I will lose out on learning valuable information."

Your job is to understand the character's inner life and make it real for yourself and the audience. What is my character experiencing? What is happening with my character? What is my character's reality? These are questions to ask yourself to help figure out the inner life. It is very helpful to ask these questions in character and in the first person. For example, "What am I experiencing?"

OBJECTIVES

Human beings always want something. It can be something basic, like food or shelter. Or it can be something more complex, like acceptance or spiritual freedom. What do I want? What do I need? What do I not have that I want? What is the other character doing that I don't like? What is the other character not doing that I want him to do? These are questions to ask yourself to help figure out your objective. Objective, need and want are synonymous terms used frequently in the acting world.

If you are working on a play or film with multiple scenes, your character has an overall objective that he is trying to achieve during the whole play or film. Also, in each scene, your character has an objective specific to that scene. The objective in that scene is tied, in some way, to the overall objective.

If the play or film on which you are working (no matter the length) does not have scenes or act breaks, your character still has an overall objective. You have to look for transitions within the script where the character's objective might change. For example, your character may have an interaction with his mother. The mother exits. Your character's sister enters and your character interacts with her. It is very likely that your character has a different objective in each interaction.

Your objective should be active: "I want to get a piece of pizza." "I want to be accepted by my new friends at school."

BEATS AND ACTIONS

Every scene and monologue should be broken down into beats. A beat is defined as a change in tone. More specifically, a beat is an action. An action is a tactic that a character uses in order to obtain his objective. An action is expressed as an action verb.

If my objective is to "get a piece of pizza," then I may enter the kitchen and beg my mom for pizza. "Mom, may I please have a piece of pizza? Please?" If she says no, then I may pout. "I never get what I want." If she continues to deny my need for pizza, I may scold her. "You're a terrible mom and everybody knows it." Guilt her. "It's just so sad when a good person like me is denied the simple pleasures in life." Finally, I may threaten her. "I'm calling the department of social services and reporting you. I hope my new parents are nice and that the government isn't too hard on you." By the end of the scene, I either get what I want or I don't. Working this hard for a piece of pizza is a little over the top. However, it is a good example of using different tactics or actions in order to achieve an objective. Hopefully, you can see that making strong choices—to beg, to pout, to scold, to guilt, to threaten—helps give weight to the scene. Most likely, this pizza scene is comedic.

The beats will help prevent whatever it is you are working on from becoming monotonous, boring and redundant. A character, like a human being, tries different tactics in order to get what he wants. It would be very boring to watch me beg my mom for pizza for eight minutes. It becomes more interesting, and maybe funny, to watch me try different tactics. All great writers know these concepts and all great pieces of writing have objectives, beats and actions built into them. It is the actor's job to analyze the writing and figure out the author's intention.

A strong objective or action is something that I can act. I know what it means to beg for something and I can act that easily. Choosing a weak objective or action is common. "I am going to talk to my mom about pizza." "I am going to tell my mom I want pizza." Those are weak objectives. They are too general. Instead, "I am going to pressure my mom into giving me a piece of pizza." You must find a way to express the objective and actions so that they make sense to you. Strong objectives come from strong choices.

An objective can be an expression of an inner need. "I am desperate for a piece of pizza. I am starving. If I don't get pizza, I am going to fall apart."

Or it can be expressed as something that is interpersonal. "I have to get my mom to give me a piece of pizza. She is the only person who can save me."

Some or all of your actions may come from behavior you exhibit. "I will pout if my mom doesn't give me pizza." Your action is "to pout." You can pout by sitting on the floor and crossing your arms. Some or all of your actions may be interpersonal. "I am going to beg my mom for pizza." Your action is "to beg." You can beg by standing on a chair and clasping your hands. Whatever the case, you want something from someone else and you are dependent on his or her response. The response you get propels you into the next beat. You have an effect on the person with whom you are interacting and in turn that person affects you. By the end of the scene, play or film, you have either gotten what you want or you haven't.

Again, a beat is defined as a change in tone. More specifically, a beat is an action. A beat can be short or long. It can be one line, one moment or three pages.

This is a list of action verbs. It is not a definitive list.

Advise	Direct	Motivate
Aid	Dissect	Nurture
Amend	Educate	Praise
Authorize	Encourage	Raise
Belittle	Enforce	Repair
Boost	Enlighten	Serve
Capture	Entertain	Scold
Coach	Examine	Shame
Counsel	Guide	Strengthen
Comfort	Guilt	Submit
Correct	Help	Stimulate
Critique	Inform	Teach
Debate	Instruct	Test
Defend	Judge	Threaten
Defer	Lead	Transform
Defy	Lecture	Validate
Destroy		

EXAMPLE

Overall Objective—to make myself feel better about losing a dance competition

Scene Objective—to pressure my mom into giving me a piece of pizza

Actions—to beg, to pout, to scold, to guilt, to threaten

Objectives, beats and actions are built into every film and play just as they are built into everything we do in real life. We may or may not be aware of our objectives, beats and actions in real life. The characters we play may or may not be aware of their objectives, beats and actions. But, we as actors, are aware of our character's objectives, beats and actions.

In addition to figuring out the action within each beat, you analyze the inner life of the character within each beat. You develop an interpretation of what the character is experiencing from moment to moment.

INNER LIFE, OBJECTIVE AND SUBTEXT

The inner life, objective and subtext are closely related. All three have equal weight and all three are necessary in order to bring a character to life.

If your objective is to get a piece of pizza, then your inner life (or your reality) is that you are hungry. Create the hunger. Understand your objective, "I am going to force my mom to give me a piece of pizza." Your line of dialogue is, "I could never have another piece of pizza again and be fine." Your subtext is, "If you don't give me pizza right now, I will fall apart."

Avoid focusing on the emotions involved. We, as actors, are aware of how the character is feeling. However, while we are in character, going for emotion leads to pushing, overacting and bad acting.

Figuring out the inner life of the character, finding the right objective and figuring out the subtext is complicated and challenging. It usually takes extensive thought and rehearsal to find out what works. Sometimes, if we're lucky, it comes to us quickly. It is not about what is right or wrong. The goal is to find out what works. Two people playing the role of Hamlet may have two different interpretations. One actor may decide that Hamlet is mentally unstable at the beginning of the play and gradually loses his mind throughout the play. Another actor may have an interpretation that Hamlet, at the top of the play, is devastated about his father dying and his mother marrying his uncle, but he is not mentally unstable. He starts to lose his mind when he learns that his uncle killed his father. If the interpretation works, that is all that matters.

What should you focus on first? The inner life? The objective? This very important question will be addressed later in this book. As mentioned before, you cannot understand the subtext until you understand the character's inner life and the character's objective.

CHAPTER 6

GUIDANCE

IN THE MOMENT

Trust your choices. When acting, you are "in the moment." You are not thinking about your choices. You understand all of the given circumstances of the scene: "who am I," "where am I," "what is happening" and "what is my relationship to the other person or people in the scene?" You know your inner life. You know your objective and the actions you are going to take to achieve your objective. You know the subtext of the scene. You understand all of this information and trust that, like a sponge, you have soaked it up. When you take the stage or step in front of the camera, everything you do is motored by this information. You are in character. You are "in the moment."

You can't think about the given circumstances, all of the choices you have made and all of the details of your character while you are acting. It is too much to think about all at once. Your goal is to experience something while acting. You do not want to be in your head. Being "in the moment" means that you are in character and focusing on listening and responding.

Before the scene, you do a preparation in order to get into character (detailed in Chapter 7). During the scene, you are in character and listening to the other person or people on stage. You are responding to whatever is communicated to you verbally and nonverbally. Whatever is communicated to you verbally and nonverbally has an effect on you and propels you into the next beat.

In acting, just as in life, you go after what you want because of something inside of you. You are then affected by the response you get. In a film, you want to get a good grade on a book report because your parents do not think you are working hard enough in school. You believe that you have been working hard, but your English teacher, whom you admire and respect, is too tough. You want to prove yourself to your parents and your teacher. You know you're smart and you know you are a hard worker. You take great pride in your scholastic achievement. You work hard on the report and hand it in. Your teacher does not give you the grade you think you deserve. You go to your teacher. You defend your ideas in the report and praise your teacher for helping you become a more analytical thinker and writer. She eventually sees that your report contains original ideas. She gives you a higher grade. You celebrate by making copies of the report and distributing it to everyone in your family at dinner that night.

JUDGING YOUR CHARACTER

Avoid judging your character. Everybody behaves with the best intentions. We all do what we think is right at the time. We may, as the actor, understand that a character is behaving badly or with evil intentions. However, we must, as the character, believe that what we are doing is right. Some characters are self-aware. Some are oblivious to the fact that they are behaving in a destructive manner. This level of self-awareness gives depth to a character.

Does Michael, in *The Godfather*, know that he has crossed a line at the end of the film when he lies to his wife, Kay? We, as the audience, know that deceiving his wife is dishonorable. We, as the actor, know that this action signifies that he has transformed from a law-abiding and moral man into a ruthless and cunning head of a mafia family. If you are playing Michael, it is up to you to decide how aware you are that what you are doing is wrong. It is not helpful for you, as the actor, to judge Michael. If anything, you must understand that Michael has been pushed into this position and he is doing whatever it takes to save his family. If it means that he has to lie to his wife, then that is what he has to do.

Take it a step further and fall in love with your character. Have compassion for your character. If you are playing Michael, you should understand him and care for him. You understand that he is in a complex position and he must take action that shatters his moral compass.

SCRIPT ANALYSIS AND REHEARSAL

"Analyzing a script" and "breaking down a script" are terms frequently used in the acting world. They are synonymous terms.

The first thing you should do is read the script as many times as possible. The more times you read the script, the better. You will have a deeper understanding of the author's intention after the fiftieth time you read the script than you did the first time.

Write down your initial impressions. You will start to have ideas about objectives and the character's inner life. You will start to analyze the relationships and discover any physical traits the character has. As you move forward, you will start to test out your ideas in rehearsal, by yourself or with your cast. Most of the rehearsal process is done on your own. This is when you really test your ideas. A rehearsal with a cast, if you have a rehearsal, is for when you've narrowed down your choices to your best ones. You go to rehearsal and test out your choices. If your choices work, that's great. If not, you go home and try something else. Then go back to your cast rehearsal with your new choices and try them. By opening night of a stage performance or the first take on a film, you have tested everything out and you are confident that it is going to work.

At some point during the time when you're reading the script, you should write or type out your lines. Do not include punctuation. People do not speak according to punctuation. We do not pause when there should be a period or question mark. We pause in order to take a breath, to find our thoughts or if we are overcome with emotion. Taking out the punctuation is a great way to avoid falling into the trap of saying the lines in a pattern. Without punctuation, you are free to say the words organically. Punctuation is necessary in order to make a script legible. It can be a hindrance when going through the process of finding your character's voice and expressing your character's thoughts and feelings. Also, when writing out your lines, only write out the other character's first few words and last few words. The character's last few words are your cue words. These are the only words you need to know in order to say your lines. Cutting out the other character's lines will also help in rehearsal. Since you're not hearing those lines over and over on your own, you will hear them in your cast rehearsal and perhaps listen a little more intently.

Remove all stage directions such as "moves slowly toward the pool" or "he picks up the glass and throws it." Remove all acting directions such as "angrily" or "with a slight smile." Stage directions and acting directions in a script sometimes have been added because they are what worked for a specific theater production. Those directions do not serve you. In general, stage and acting directions in a script for a play or film may help in understanding the author's intention, but ultimately you will decide how to play the scene. Remove all stage and acting directions.

This is Hamlet's famous "To be or not to be" speech the way it is commonly punctuated. There are no original copies of the text in existence. Numerous people, scholars, for example, have added punctuation as they see fit.

> Hamlet: To be, or not to be—that is the question:
> Whether 'tis nobler in the mind to suffer
> The slings and arrows of outrageous fortune
> Or to take arms against a sea of troubles,
> And by opposing end them. To die—to sleep—
> No more; and by a sleep to say we end
> The heartache, and the thousand natural shocks
> That flesh is heir to. 'Tis a consummation
> Devoutly to be wish'd. To die—to sleep.
> To sleep—perchance to dream: ay, there's the rub!

Here is the speech after I have read it and am ready to start memorizing it. Iambic pentameter and scansion are certainly considerations when working on Shakespeare. Scanning is figuring out what syllables are stressed and unstressed. With this in mind, I can remove the punctuation and memorize the speech first. If I choose to make scanning part of my process, I can then work on the speech with punctuation. Some people scan and some don't. The point is, no matter what the text is, it can be very helpful to see the words without any punctuation.

> To be or not to be that is the question whether 'tis nobler in the mind to suffer the slings and arrows of outrageous fortune or to take arms against a sea of troubles and by opposing end them to die to sleep no more and by a sleep to say we end the heartache and the thousand natural shocks that flesh is heir to 'tis a consummation devoutly to be wish'd to die to sleep to sleep perchance to dream ay there's the rub

Oftentimes, a film has little or no rehearsal. For film, it is especially important to make sure that you have done extensive homework. Most of the time, you are arriving on set and you get a few times to run through a scene. Then you execute the scene. You may not get any rehearsal. However, in some cases you will have ample time to rehearse. If you are lucky, you may get six weeks of rehearsals and meet with your cast three or four times a week. Perhaps you share a farmhouse with your cast in Maine for a week. You rehearse, improvise and write letters to each other in character.

The sample on the following page is what your script should look like after working on it. Use a pencil to make notes so that you can easily erase and change your choices.

This technique can be applied to breaking down any scripted material of any length. The only difference between breaking down a monologue or a short scene and a longer piece is that in the monologue or short scene you do not have an overall objective. You do, however, have an objective. The monologue or short scene can, from there, be broken down into beats.

Breaking down a script is challenging and takes practice.

HIGHLIGHTERS, PENCILS AND PENS

Use a highlighter to highlight your lines. Some actors find this helpful in memorizing lines or simply being able to find their lines during rehearsals or auditions.

Always have at least two pens and two pencils with you at classes, auditions and rehearsals. If one breaks or runs out of ink, you'll have an extra. Be ready to take notes that a director or teacher gives. Write down a thought you have immediately, before you forget it. At an audition, you may be asked to sign in and fill out an information card. Use a pen.

REHEARSAL TECHNIQUES

There are many rehearsal techniques that you can use on your own and with the actors in your cast. Begin by using these techniques at home; this is where most of your character work should take place. Use rehearsals with the rest of the cast to test the choices you've worked out. If a choice works with the other actors, you move on to another aspect of your character on your own. If your choice does not work or it needs adjusting, you go home and rehearse. Below are some rehearsal techniques.

Objective
- ~~Get pizza.~~ Make my Mom get me pizza.
- Feel better.

Inner Life
- Lost dance competition.
- ~~Very disappointed~~ Crushed.
- Jealous of my friend who won.

SCENE 3

(Marvin enters the kitchen. Mom is reading a book.)

MARVIN
Thank you for making chicken and mashed potatoes for dinner. That's my favorite.

Action

MOM
You're welcome. I hope you feel better.

I hate chicken and mashed potatoes.

Praise

MARVIN
You're a good mom. The best.

Inner Life

MOM
Thanks.

You were wrong.

MARVIN
I do feel better. You were right. It will take some time, but it's not the end of the world. I'll have a piece of pizza and let time heel my wounds.

← Signifies beat

MOM
No. I don't want you to have pizza. We're eating in a little bit.

MARVIN
Beg Please. Pizza is my favorite thing in the world and it would help.

This is humiliating.

MOM
That's your sister's pizza. I told her I would save the leftovers.

MARVIN
Great. Nothing ever works out for me.

I hate my life.

MOM
Don't be dramatic.

MARVIN
Guilt I have nothing. All I have is this certificate of participation from the dance competition. I'll hang it next to my participation award from soccer.

MOM
Marvin, find something to read or watch a movie.

MARVIN
I don't feel good. I feel like I'm going to faint. I haven't eaten since this morning. Low blood sugar. Help.
Scare

She's never going to believe I'm actually sick. I've gone too far.

1. Improvisation is when you are in character and you are saying whatever you want. You do not adhere to the structure of the scene or the words that are written. An improvisation can last as long as you want. Improvisation can be done on your own or with other actors.

   Before an improvisation, decide if you are going to explore an aspect of the character's inner life, your objective or the relationship to the other person or people in the scene. An improvisation can be set at the same time and place as the written scene. An improvisation can be set before or after the written scene. The improv can be an event that is discussed in the play or film, but not seen in the play or film. The improv can be set before or after the play or film.

   For example, it is written in the play that your character tripped and fell in front of a large group of people at school last year. Everyone laughed and people still tease your character about it. It was a very embarrassing event. Your character feels insecure and always makes an extra effort to be sure that he doesn't fall again. Perhaps you, the actor, decide that the character specifically feels insecure about his coordination. That is what sticks out to you about the given circumstances. You now have to create the reality of feeling insecure about your coordination. This reality affects everything your character does, from the way he walks to the way he interacts with other people. You, the actor, can work on this at home. You get ready in the morning taking extra precautions to not be clumsy or, even worse, fall. You rearrange your bookcase. You have to get on a ladder and keep your balance in order to reach the top of the bookcase. You have to stack books and carry them across the room. You put on exercise clothes. You go for a run. You run backwards and then side to side. The things you can do as an actor are endless. Your goal is to create the reality of feeling insecure about your coordination. You also have a physical adjustment of being clumsy. You take what you have worked on in your improvisation and see if it creates interesting behavior during your rehearsal with other actors. If it works, you can then focus on something else. You now have this ready to go whenever you get into character. You also have a prior life that exists outside of the play. If, while you were running, you actually did fall, then this experience will undoubtedly feed your character work.

2. Paraphrasing is when you adhere to the structure of the scene, but you do not say the words as written. You say something close to the words, but you use your own words. If you are rehearsing at home by yourself, you play off an imaginary person.

3. When improvising or paraphrasing, you can speak out your character's inner monologue. An inner monologue is when you are in character and saying out loud the character's thoughts and feelings. In character, you say out loud what you are experiencing or your objective. You talk about how you feel about the other characters. Essentially, you explore every aspect of your character and the given circumstances.

   For example, if I am playing the guy who is clumsy, I might decide that during my rehearsal at home I am going to wash dishes. I can do the activity with the goal of making discoveries about my character's objective. It might go a little something like this. Again, I say this out loud:

   "Everybody thinks I'm clumsy. I'm not clumsy. I am very coordinated. I have not fallen in three days. Maybe I am clumsy. I've always bumped into things and tripped and I have trouble catching balls. I'm clumsy. I feel like I don't have full control over my body. My hands don't do exactly what I want them to do. I trip on things and I don't know why. Don't chip this dish. Don't chip this dish. Don't chip this dish. Handle it carefully. Slow down and place it very carefully on the counter. That was good. See, I can be graceful. I am going to become coordinated. I will do drills in order to train myself. I will prove to everyone that I am not clumsy. I am excited now. My heart is racing. I have a ton of energy. Jenny will never make fun of me again. I wish we were better friends and that she didn't tease me. I am going to prove to Jenny and everyone that I am not clumsy."

   The inner monologue can be used in rehearsal with other actors. Obviously, the other actors should be aware that you are using an inner monologue. Also, while the main focus may be exploring the objective, of course many other aspects of the character come into play while doing an improvisation. Discoveries about the objective, aspects of the inner life and how you feel about other characters are made. Having a main focus simply gives you a place to start.

You can also use the inner monologue to speak out what you, the actor, are experiencing. For example, while rehearsing you say, "This isn't going well. I don't understand this character. I don't know why this character is here. I don't know why this character wouldn't leave. I need to figure this out." Obviously, if you are in rehearsal with other actors and a director, those people should be aware and accepting of using an inner monologue in this way.

4. There are many more effective rehearsal techniques that have been developed over the years by acting teachers and actors, such as writing in a journal as the character and being interviewed by someone else while in character.

BLOCKING

Blocking is the process that determines where and when you move on the stage or film location. It also involves the use of props. Some directors like to block everything out on paper and will tell you what to do. Other directors will give you full freedom to move as you wish in rehearsal and then see what is working. Others do a little of both. There is not a right or wrong way to block. Usually, the blocking becomes locked by opening night or the first take and you are responsible for having it memorized.

For the stage, you need to know where to go when someone tells you to go upstage right or downstage left.

The notations you make in your script for blocking look like this:

Downstage Right—DR

Upstage Left—UL

It doesn't really matter what you write in your script as long as you understand your notations.

STAGE DIAGRAM

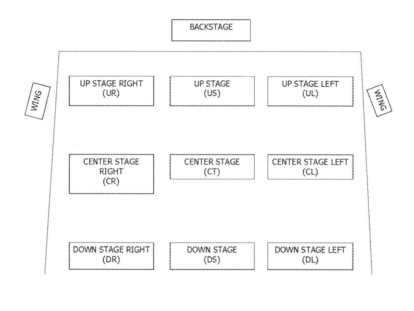

BACKSTAGE

UP STAGE RIGHT (UR)	UP STAGE (US)	UP STAGE LEFT (UL)
CENTER STAGE RIGHT (CR)	CENTER STAGE (CT)	CENTER STAGE LEFT (CL)
DOWN STAGE RIGHT (DR)	DOWN STAGE (DS)	DOWN STAGE LEFT (DL)

WING   WING

AUDIENCE

THE FOURTH WALL

The fourth wall is an imaginary wall downstage. It is the dividing line between you and the audience.

If the play or scene is set in an interior location, then the fourth wall is an imaginary wall in that location that closes up the room. If the location is an exterior space, the imaginary line still exists. However, the location extends to the back wall of the theater. The back wall of the theater is the horizon of the exterior location.

In both cases, when you look out toward the audience, you look up and over the heads of the audience members. You do not make eye contact with the audience. If it is written that you make eye contact with the audience or that you speak to the audience, then you are breaking the fourth wall. If you speak directly to a camera, you are breaking the fourth wall.

CHEATING OUT

Cheating out is defined as positioning yourself so that you can be seen by the audience or camera. As opposed to speaking to another actor in profile, keeping your back to the audience or camera, or directly facing the audience or camera, you cheat out in order speak to another actor while remaining in view of the audience or camera. Most of the time, but not always, you cheat out.

When you cross the stage and turn, you cheat out by turning toward the audience. You do not turn upstage.

When you are speaking to another actor, you do not always have to be facing that actor. You can be downstage right and he can be upstage center. You can look out toward the fourth wall and deliver your lines. You can turn to him every so often. You do not want to deliver all your lines to him with your back to the audience. This is considered upstaging yourself. Generally, you want to be on the same plane, or close to it, with the actor to whom you are speaking.

If you are upstage and the actor to whom you are speaking is downstage, you are upstaging the other actor. You are forcing him to turn to you. He is then upstaging himself. In general, it creates an ugly stage picture.

The rules of cheating out and upstaging are not set in stone. There are exceptions.

However, your instinct should be to avoid upstaging yourself and others.

Another form of upstaging is when you do something physical or verbal while another actor is speaking or doing something nonverbal. This is also known as stealing focus. You should be in character at all times, but do not steal focus from another character.

THE DIRECTOR

The director's main job with relation to an actor is to inspire him. Ideally, the director and you should share the same interpretation of the character and the play or film. If possible, you should find out before being cast if you share the same interpretation. Of course this is not always possible. If the director and you are at odds with each other, the process becomes very difficult. If the director is imposing his ideas on you, the results can be disastrous. If you find yourself working in a toxic environment, you do your best to get through it. The truth is when you are young and starting out, you usually take whatever opportunity comes your way. Once you have built up your resume, you can afford to be more selective with the projects on which you work and the people with whom you work.

CHAPTER 7

ACTING TECHNIQUES

MEMORIZING LINES

If you have a great memory, you might read the script once and the lines will stick in your mind. You can recite them without a problem. If you have trouble memorizing lines, there are many things you can do. Reading the script over and over will help. Here are some memorization techniques:

1. Read the lines and say them out loud without looking at the script, either on your own or with someone.

2. Put a piece of paper over your script. Move the paper down and read the other character's line. Then say your line. Move the paper to the other character's next line.

3. Write or type out the other character's lines. Leave space to write your lines. If it's a monologue, write it out.

4. Record the other character's lines into a recording device. Leave enough time to say your lines. Play the recording and test yourself.

5. Tape the scene to a wall and read it. There is something about being on your feet and reading it out loud that helps.

6. Make it the first thing you read when you wake up and the last thing you read when you go to bed. Read it throughout the day as many times as possible.

7. There are helpful apps available for phones that incorporate some or all of the techniques above.

The idea is to know the lines so well that you don't have to think about the words when you are acting. While acting, instead of trying to think about what you say next, you are thinking about why you are saying what has been written.

If you have trouble memorizing lines, it is important to develop your ability. In professional situations, you are expected to know your lines perfectly and must sometimes learn new ones quickly. In any situation, there is the possibility that lines will be cut, added or rearranged.

You can develop your memory by memorizing short pieces from a monologue or poem or anything that interests you. Start by memorizing a very short piece and practice reciting it multiple times a day. Recite that piece every day for a week. Then build on the amount you memorize as you shorten the deadline for memorizing it. If you work on pieces from Shakespeare, in the course of a year you will have memorized some of the greatest words ever written and then have them at your disposal for the rest of your life. Start with something simple and then challenge yourself at your own pace.

Whether memorizing lines comes easily or takes tremendous effort, avoid getting into a rhythm when reciting the words. Lines should be memorized and recited in monotone in order to avoid falling into automatic rhythms. Ironically, people who have an easy time memorizing lines are hindered by this ability. They often have to work to avoid getting caught in a rhythm.

BREATHING

An actor articulates his words and speaks at an audible volume. He has control of his breath. His breath has power.

Proper control of breath requires diaphragmatic breathing. The diaphragm is a muscle located at the base of the lungs.

BREATHING EXERCISE

Do the following exercise in order to learn how to activate your diaphragm.

1. Lie down.
2. Your knees can be raised or flat on the floor.
3. Put one hand on your stomach and one hand on your chest.
4. Inhale through your nose or your mouth.

5. When you inhale, you should feel the hand on your stomach rise. Your chest should be still.

6. Exhale through your nose or your mouth.

7. When you exhale, you should feel the hand on your stomach fall. When you inhale, your lungs fill with air. When you exhale, your lungs deflate.

8. Inhale and exhale ten times. Do three or more rounds of this.

9. See if you can keep your concentration on counting. If you lose count, start over.

10. Inhale and let out a sound as you exhale. The sound should be an "ahhhhh" sound. The sound should be powered by your diaphragm. You should feel very little, if any, vibrations in your chest and throat.

11. Inhale and exhale until you are comfortable with this form of breathing. Some people naturally breathe with their diaphragm. Some people have to practice in order to do it properly.

Once you are comfortable with diaphragmatic breath, do the following exercises:

1. Execute diaphragmatic breath while standing.

2. Inhale and count to ten. Exhale. Inhale and count to ten again. Exhale. Repeat as many times as you want.

3. Count to ten. Over-enunciate the words. Stretch your lips as you speak. Repeat as many times as you want.

4. Count to ten. Play with pitch. Start high and go low. Start low and go high. Go up and down and all around. Repeat as many times as you want.

5. Inhale and count as high as you can until you are out of breath. When you are reaching the end of your breath, do not struggle or push to get the number out. Stay in control. Be aware of when you are running out of breath. When you feel you are running out of breath, inhale and either start over at one or continue where you left off.

    The key is to be in control of your breath. Your goal is to count as high as you can on one breath. But you should not rush or force the numbers out. With practice, you will count higher and higher.

6. Inhale and count to ten or higher. While you are counting, play with volume. Pretend that you are filling a five-hundred-seat theater. Pretend that you are on camera in a close-up shot and a microphone is one foot from your face.

7. Inhale and say a speech, read from a book, read from a magazine or say anything you want. Inhale and exhale freely while speaking or reading what you have chosen.

Start to experiment with your breath. See how long you can speak with one breath. See if you can control a series of short breaths.

The goal is to make breathing from the diaphragm second nature. Practice it in real life.

While acting, you should not be thinking about your breath. You are in the moment. If you need to take a breath in order to get oxygen, then take a breath. If you are in an emotional state and your impulse is to get a large amount of information out on one long breath, then you can. If you need to get a short amount of information out on one explosive breath, then you have that ability.

BEING CENTERED

Being centered means that your body is free of tension. It is balanced. Your body is ready for physical and vocal demands.

Find Your Center

Follow these directions in order to find your center:

1. Stand with your feet hip distance apart.

2. Close your eyes.

3. Let your arms fall to your sides.

4. Put your weight on the balls of your feet. Feel a little bit of weight on your big toes.

5. Lock your knees and release. Lock your knees and release. Lock your knees and leave them released.

6. Let your chin fall to your chest.

7. Roll over, one vertebra at a time, until you are hanging upside down. You are bent over at the waist. The top of your head is pointed toward the ground. Your arms are either touching the floor or dangling. You do not need to touch the floor. This is not about being flexible.

8. Your knees should be unlocked. You should feel a nice stretch in your low back.

9. Check and see if you are holding up your head with your neck. If you are, let your head go.

10. Wiggle your fingers. Your hands. Your arms.

11. Gently sway from side to side.

12. Stop swaying.

13. Let out a breath. Take as many breaths as you wish.

14. When you are ready, stand up. Come up slowly, one vertebra at a time, until you are standing upright.

15. Your knees should be unlocked.

16. Your hips are sitting comfortably over your feet.

17. Your shoulders are not pulled back and they are not pushed forward.

18. Your chin is neither pushed out nor tilted down.

19. Your head is balanced on top of the spine.

20. Your jaw is unclenched.

21. Take a breath.

Your goal is to get to the point where you can find your center without rolling over and up. It may feel good to roll over and up, but you can get to the point that you don't have to do it in order to find your center. Be centered at all times in your everyday life. It should be second nature.

Being centered and diaphragmatic breath are closely related. You cannot be centered without executing diaphragmatic breath, and vice versa.

RELAXATION AND CONCENTRATION

Relaxation and concentration are two elements that form the foundation of acting.

Relaxation

We are relaxed when we act. Our bodies are free of tension. Tension is defined as unnecessary energy.

We all walk around with a certain amount of tension. We literally lock our muscles in reaction to good and bad news, exciting and uncomfortable situations, or exhilarating and terrifying events. This is natural behavior.

As actors, we release our own tension so that we can freely express what our character is experiencing.

Concentration

We ignite and maintain our full concentration at will.

Our ability to concentrate is fine-tuned. In rehearsal and performance, our power of concentration is strong enough to firmly grip the choices we have made about our character, the situation and the relationship. We trust that our grip is so strong and secure that we can then loosen our clasp and be in the moment.

Relaxation and Concentration Exercise

Here is an exercise that will help release tension and engage your concentration:

1. Find your center. Breathe.

2. Keep your eyes closed.

3. Think about your day from the moment you woke up until this moment.

4. Think about everything you thought, touched, tasted, smelled and heard. Be as specific as possible.

5. Listen to the sounds you hear right now. Accept these sounds. Accept that you may hear new noises during this exercise. Accept that during a class, rehearsal, audition or performance you may hear an unexpected noise. You may feel the floor vibrate or the ceiling shake. You may smell food. You may see someone move in your peripheral vision. Anything can happen. Accept that.

6. How do you feel right now? Are you in a good mood? A bad mood? Hot? Cold? Tired? Hungry? Any aches or pains?

7. What are your plans today? What are you going to eat? Where are you going? Are you excited about anything? Worried about anything?

8. How was the past week? What went well? What didn't go well?

9. What are you doing tomorrow? Are you excited about tomorrow? Dreading tomorrow?

10. In general, what is occupying your mind? Are you excited or looking forward to anything? Are you anxious or worried about anything?

11. Understand that you have addressed a significant number of possible distractions. Understand that you can think about these distractions later. After your class, rehearsal, audition or performance, you can figure out what you are going to have for dinner or think about the details of the event you are dreading. You can stay concentrated for as long as you want.

12. While you are acting, you may think about something that takes you out of the moment, a distraction. This will inevitably happen. It is possible that the distraction will feed your acting. Or it may take you out of the moment. But you now know that your brain has acknowledged what is going on with you. You have the capability to let the distraction come and go without taking you out of the moment.

Use this exercise word for word if you like it. If you want to, change the order or wording to suit your needs. Record it on a recording device so that you can play it back for yourself.

TENSION RELEASE EXERCISE

Here is an exercise you can do in order to release tension.

1. Find your center.

2. Squeeze your toes.

3. Squeeze your calves.

4. Squeeze your thighs.

5. Squeeze your rear end.

6. Squeeze your stomach.

7. Squeeze your chest.

8. Squeeze your hands.

9. Squeeze your forearms.

10. Squeeze your biceps.

11. Squeeze your shoulders.

12. Squeeze your neck.

13. Squeeze your face.

14. Keep everything squeezed.

15. Let it go.

16. Let out a long breath with an "ahhhhh" sound.

17. Start at your toes and quickly work your way up to your face. Let it go. Let out a breath with sound.

PREPARATION

Prepare your body physically, mentally and vocally before you rehearse, audition or perform. Do it at home, at school, at a theater or on a film set. You may need thirty minutes in order to prepare or just five.

1. Find your center.

2. Do the relaxation and concentration exercise.

3. Release tension.

4. Test your voice.

5. Get into character.
   a. Think about your choices.
   b. Think about whatever it is you need to think about in order to take on the character's inner life.

There are many different and effective relaxation, concentration and voice exercises. Most exercises have variations. In the end, the only thing that matters is that you like an exercise and that it works for you.

THE ACTOR'S MAP

The following image pares down and lays out the components that make up the artistic aspects of the actor and acting. This is the "Actor's Map."

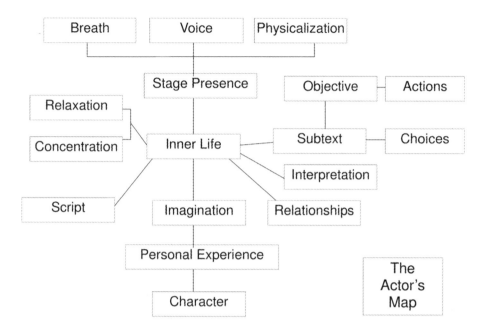

"WHERE DO I START?"

A fundamental question is, "Where do I start?" This has been the topic of debate for as long as actors have taken the stage. "Do I work on creating the inner life of the character?" Or "do I focus on my objective, relationship and physical attributes?" Beyond figuring out where to start is the question "What is most important?"

If you ask a variety of actors, directors, acting teachers and acting theorists, you'll get a variety of answers. In the end, every actor must experiment and figure out his own approach. What works for one person won't necessarily work for another person.

ACTING TECHNIQUE

Since the Greek writer Thespis first put an actor on the stage around 500 B.C.E., people have theorized and argued about acting technique. Aristotle, Francois Delsarte, Konstantin Stanislavsky, Vsevolod Meyerhold, Lee Strasberg, Stella Adler, Sanford Meisner and many others have all theorized about acting. Sometimes, there has been agreement. Most of the time there has been disagreement. At the core of the debate is how an actor should bring a character to life. Some people believe that an actor should use his powers of imagination to draw upon past experiences. Some people believe that an actor should use his powers of imagination to invent details. Some people believe both approaches together are effective. Some believe that you can put on a fake nose and wig in order to get into character. Some believe that an actor can simply read a scene or script, understand it and execute it using inspiration. Some believe in using a combination of all of these approaches and perhaps an approach not specified in this book.

Almost everybody agrees that an actor's responsibility is to bring a character to life by creating real and believable behavior.

PUTTING IT ALL TOGETHER AND MOVING FORWARD

The exercises in this book are intended to help you explore a character with very simple dialogue. After getting comfortable with making and executing strong choices (perhaps even mastering the process), then it is time to work with more complex dialogue. The next stage is developing your capability of figuring out an author's intention. Your job is to figure out the author's intention and then develop an original interpretation. Your interpretation is one of the things that distinguishes you as an actor.

Breaking down a script, analyzing a character and some of the other concepts and guidance discussed in this book can be perceived as too academic, too intellectual, over analytical and perhaps mechanical. Some people might believe some of the concepts and guidance inhibit spontaneity and instincts. Take into consideration that after practice and a period of time, you will gain a firm understanding of these fundamental aspects of acting and the whole process of acting will become organic. In order to allow your spontaneity and instincts to function you have to at least know that you are headed in the right direction. For example, after a certain period of time, you may decide that when you analyze a script you like to write down all of your choices. You decide that you will always use this strategy. Or perhaps you will decide that you don't need to write down your choices and that you can do it in your head. Every actor usually develops his own approach. If you analyze a script and write down your choices in detail, you are creating a blueprint. Nothing is set in stone. There is always room to make discoveries and change your choices as you move forward in the rehearsal process. Instincts guide you through the whole process. But, you have to be conscious of your instincts and confident that your instincts are leading you in the direction of truthful artistic expression.

This book does not present an acting technique. I do not anywhere in this book explain specifically how to create real behavior. I am simply presenting the major concepts that most acting techniques employ. I have led you along a path of using your imagination to create behavior. Imagination can be used to draw upon past experiences, invent details or both. In the section, "Inner Life, Objective and Subtext", I wrote "create the hunger." The big question is, "How do I create the hunger?" This is what acting theorists have been contemplating and debating since Thespis. The various uses of imagination that I have touched upon are what most acting techniques use to "create the hunger." Most people believe that learning a technique is vital to become an artist of the highest caliber.

ACTING CLASSES AND TRAINING

The exercises and ideas discussed in this book are suitable for individual study, a school classroom or theater school.

There are excellent acting schools all over the world. If your interest level and schedule allow for one class a week, then you should have no problem finding a knowledgeable teacher. If you are interested in dedicating more time to acting training, then you should look for a school with a curriculum that includes acting technique, camera technique, audition technique, improvisation classes, movement classes, dance classes, stage combat classes, singing classes, voice/speech/accent training, theatre and film history, film analysis, the business of acting and performance opportunities.

This book touches upon some basic concepts. It is important to understand that this is only the beginning.

CONTROL

Good acting is good acting. It doesn't matter how you get there as long as you get there. You are in control of how you feel about your performance. As long as you are happy with what you do, it doesn't matter what relatives, friends, teachers, directors, critics or anybody else thinks. You will never please everybody. You are in control. You are an artist.

THE ACTOR AS ARTIST

Being an actor does not always mean that you strive to be on Broadway or in Hollywood feature films. There are many actors who pursue their art in various ways while working other jobs and pursuing other interests.

Many actors do not measure their success by how much money they make, how many recognizable credits they have, the famous actors with whom they have worked or the awards they have won.

There are opportunities to learn, hone and execute your craft in every part of the world. If an area is lacking opportunities, help create an artistic community. In Chapter 9 of this book, I address the principles important in producing your own work.

As a beginning actor, your focus should be on developing as an artist. An artist expresses original ideas. Or he expresses old ideas in an original way. His work may or may not be something that is suitable for the mass market. An artist is happy and satisfied when he has created something that is a true reflection of what he thinks, feels and believes.

At the core, the question is not whether one is a professional or an amateur actor. The question is whether one is an artist.

An artist is uninhibited by external forces. He is not dependent on or influenced by money, praise, recognition, fame, or criticism. An artist is one who is free to observe and explore the world and then express his thoughts and feelings about what he has experienced. This freedom is integral to pure artistic expression.

A good teacher, mentor or observer can provide invaluable feedback, guidance and encouragement. But that person, in the end, does not bear the responsibility for what you create.

We measure success, as artists, by gauging the pleasure we achieve from our work. If we believe that we have expressed ourselves truthfully, then we can achieve an extraordinary sense of satisfaction and sometimes an unrivaled euphoria.

CHAPTER 8

FILM ACTING

A common misconception is that an actor has to be "bigger" when acting on stage and "smaller" when acting on camera. There is no difference between acting on stage and acting on camera. With proper control of your breath, you will have no problem with projection and articulation in a large theater or in front of a camera with a microphone five inches from your face.

On stage, there is usually some sort of distance between you and the audience. On camera, in a close-up shot, the audience (which is essentially the camera) is very close to your face. The camera picks up every little movement. If you have tension in your face, purse your lips, breathe heavily or blink excessively, the camera will pick it up and these bad habits will become distractions for the audience. There is a difference between an actor exhibiting behavior and a character exhibiting behavior. A well-trained eye knows whether tension, lip pursing, heavy breathing and excessive blinking are a result of the actor experiencing something or the character experiencing something. A casual audience member subconsciously knows the difference. Bad habits are amplified on camera.

Earlier, I discussed the challenge that film presents with regard to rehearsal.

One of the other major challenges film presents is that a film is usually shot of out order. A play starts at the beginning, works its way to the climax and then it is over. You may have a weekend run or a six-month run. Making it real for yourself and the audience every performance is your challenge on stage.

In film, you may shoot the climax of the film on the first day. Whoever is scheduling the production does her best to make it easy on the actors.

However, in the end, it comes down to money and timing. For example, if the producer is able to get a certain location on the first day of the shoot for a great price, then she may do it even though it is the climax of the film. So we have to be ready to do any scene from the film on any day of the shoot. We have to know our character's arc and where the character is in his arc.

The "character's arc" is the character's journey. How does he think, feel and behave at the beginning of the story? How does he change, if at all, by the end of the story?

The following "Character Arc Worksheet" is an example of how to map out your character's arc when working on a film.

CHARACTER ARC WORKSHEET

Project: The Limit

General Script Analysis

- Do not like organized social activities
- Do not like school
- Prefer to learn on my own
- Pressured into competing in dance competition by Ike
- Like video games and interacting with people on the Internet
- Don't like buses

Relationships

- Mom
  - Always urging me to be more social
  - Wants me to grow up, be more mature, "act my age"
- Ike
  - Wants to hang out more
  - Thinks I'm a social outcast
  - Genuinely concerned about me but pushy with very little tact
- People at school
  - Everyone thinks I'm a little odd.

Acting Notes

- In scene 8, I have to cry.

- Dancing
  - Terrible dancer
  - Need to practice

Objectives and Inner Life for Each Scene

- Overall Objective: To have a normal social life

Scene

1. Home—playing video games
   - No dialogue
   - Objective: To win
   - Inner Life: Feeling lost, misunderstood, helpless
2. At school—lunch with Ike
   - Ike tells me he's worried about me.
   - Ike challenges me to compete in the dance competition.
   - Objective: Get Ike off my back.
   - Inner Life: I know he's right but I don't want to admit it.
3. Home with parents
   - Parents discuss my situation. They are worried about me.
   - I tell them I am going to compete in a dance competition.
   - Objective: Prove that my parents are wrong.
   - Inner Life: Taking control of the situation.

Note to Reader: This is a good start. If you were analyzing the whole script, you would continue with each scene until the end of the script.

Locations

Home—scene 1, 3, 5
School—scene 2, 4, 7
Park—scene 6
Hotel—scene 8
Garage—scene 9

Wardrobe

Note to Reader—Look at each scene and note what you are going to wear. If it is a low-budget film, you may have to provide everything you wear.

You may have to use your own clothes and buy new ones if necessary. Big-budget productions usually have a wardrobe person.

Makeup and Hair

Note to Reader—There may be a makeup and a hair person on set. You may be on your own. Whether you are male or female, you should know how to do your hair and makeup so that it looks good on camera. Hair should be kept out of your eyes. If you wear makeup, a makeup artist can help you figure out a look that works for you.

CHAPTER 9

AUDITIONING

In most cases, in order to get cast in a play or film, we have to audition. Sometimes, someone we know asks us to be in her production and we don't have to audition. If we do have to audition, a specific skill set and mindset are required.

For this section, I am going to refer to the person who is conducting the audition as the auditor. An auditor might be a teacher, director, casting director, producer or anyone else who is helping cast a project.

THE GOAL

The main goal of an audition is to prepare, execute what you have prepared and walk away without any regrets. You want to be able to say to yourself, "I did the best I could. It's out of my hands."

You do not want to walk out and say to yourself, "I should have . . ." or "I wish I had . . ." This is what we call the "elevator read." After the audition, don't get in the proverbial elevator and go over all of the things you did wrong. It is a destructive thing to do and it feels terrible. It is good to be aware of what went right and what went wrong. It is smart to know what you need to do in order to get better at auditioning. It is not productive to beat yourself up or criticize yourself.

Your focus during the audition is not on getting the part. The focus is on presenting yourself as someone who is easy to work with and professional. This is true for a school production and for a major Hollywood film. The auditor has called you in to audition or you have signed up for the audition. From the moment you enter the space where the audition is taking place, you are being observed. You never know who is in the parking lot, the lobby, the elevator or the waiting room. Somebody attached to the project is usually there. People want to work with others who conduct themselves in a mature manner. Being loud or bringing negative attention to yourself in any way can hurt your chances of getting cast.

It is impossible to know what an auditor is thinking. Don't bother trying to figure her out. She may tell you that you are the best actor she has ever seen and then you never hear from her again. She may not say a word to you or even make eye contact with you, and you find out thirty minutes later that you got the part.

AUDITION MATERIAL

There are many different circumstances you may encounter. Here are some examples:

1. You have to perform one or more monologues. These are monologues that you have chosen and prepared. You should pick a monologue from a contemporary published play or produced film. Do not pick something you have written or something obscure. Usually, the auditor will ask that the monologue be no more than two minutes long. If you are doing two monologues, sometimes the auditor will expect that one monologue will be dramatic and the other comedic. There can be a fine line between drama and comedy, so most people believe that your two monologues should simply be different in some way. Most actors have at least two monologues ready to perform at any time and in any situation. The only time you perform a classical piece such as Shakespeare is when the auditor specifically asks for a classical piece. Your monologue or monologues should be well rehearsed. An auditor is expecting a performance. An audition is not an opportunity to test out a new monologue that is unpolished.

2. You have been asked to prepare a scene from the play or screenplay that is being cast. You have had time to read the whole play or screenplay. Perhaps you have had one week, or perhaps you have had one day. Perhaps a scene has been specified, or perhaps you are asked to pick a scene.

3. You have been given a scene, oftentimes referred to as "sides," from a play or screenplay you have never read. You will not have the opportunity to read the full script unless you are given a callback, offered the part or cast. Writers, directors and producers can be very protective of their material and do not want to give out the full script. Unfortunately, people steal story ideas from other people.

4. You are given sides upon your arrival at the audition and have a short period of time to prepare. This is a cold read. When executing a cold read, make some quick choices and commit to them. It's an unnerving situation and everybody knows it. Breathe and stay focused. In any audition situation, you may be asked to do a cold read. You could be asked to read for another character. You could be asked to read a scene you have not prepared. You could be asked to read a scene you've never seen before. Be prepared for anything.

DIRECTION

In all of the situations above, you may be given direction. You may be given a physical adjustment, a character adjustment or both. You may be told to deliver a line a certain way. You may be given bad direction. Whatever the case, as in a rehearsal situation, listen to what you are told and do your best to fulfill the request. Often the director simply wants to see if you can take direction. Directors love actors who are malleable.

HOW DO I GET AN AUDITION?

There are several websites that list audition opportunities. As of the writing of this book, backstage.com and actorsaccess.com are two of those websites. (If you are not near a major city, there is most likely a website that serves your community.) You create a profile on one or both of those websites and submit yourself for theater or film projects. If the person conducting the audition wants to call you in, you will be contacted. If you are given an audition, you should show up ten minutes early. If you can't make it to the audition, contact the auditor and let her know.

Take an acting class or find places where theater and film people go. Make friends. Eventually, you'll meet someone who wants to work with you.

If you are in a major market such as New York or Los Angeles, then you can get auditions through an agent or manager. There is a section in the next chapter that explains working with agents and managers.

You should never pay to audition for a project.

PROJECT DESCRIPTION AND BREAKDOWN

Sometimes you are given enough information about the project in order to know exactly what you are getting into. Other times, you know very little. Usually, you are provided with a character description, a summary of the story and information about performance dates or filming dates. This is called a breakdown. A breakdown is used in order to convey all of the pertinent information about a project. The following is an example of a breakdown.

1 PM   John Davidson – MONDAY 9/16 – SIDES ATTACHED

The Limit	Executive Producer: Mike Marks
Short Film	Co-Executive Producer: Miguel Lants
NON-Union	Producer: Angela Davis
	Director: Miguel Lants
	Writer: Mike Marks
	N.Y. Casting Director: Meredith Lincoln
	Start Date: Sept 23
	Location: New York

Meredith Lincoln Casting
239 E 44th St. #4409
NY, NY 11901

PLEASE NOTE: We are creating a world of funny characters. Don't limit yourself to physical or racial description.

This is based on the successful off-Broadway play.

[NORMAN] 14 years old. He's outgoing and would rather stay home and play video games and read. Quick witted. Must be able to dance. Ethnicity open.

WHAT SHOULD I WEAR?

You should wear clothes that are appropriate for the character. If you are auditioning for a character who is running for student council and is about to give a speech to his fellow students, then you might wear khaki pants and a button-down shirt. If you are auditioning for a character who helps his dad out at a car repair shop, you may wear jeans and a T-shirt. You don't need to wear greasy pants and smear car grease on your face.

Don't go overboard with wardrobe. Wear something that suggests what the character might wear. You may be asked to wear something dressy or casual. Have comfortable and clean clothes available at all times. Many actors have clothes that they only use for auditions. White does not look good on camera. Some people believe black should be avoided. Simple and solid is best. Avoid wild patterns and big logos (unless they really are right for the character). Stick with solid colors in muted tones. Blues and greens work best.

APPEARANCE

You always want to look your best. Be sure that your hair is not in your face.

IN THE ROOM

When you walk into the audition, do not shake hands with the auditor. Enter the space and say hello. Engage in small talk if the auditor initiates it. The auditor is probably seeing many people that day. She probably does this every day or regularly. Some people are talkers and some aren't. Conducting an audition is tough and repetitive work. Some auditors get a thrill from meeting new people or seeing someone they know. Others are all business. Don't take it personally if someone you've met numerous times doesn't show enthusiasm when you enter.

There might be one person in the space with you. There might be twelve people in the space with you. You might be greeted warmly and introduced to everyone. Or you might walk in and find that nobody says a word to you. Whatever happens, go with the flow and be ready to start the audition when you get your cue.

If you are in a theater, the auditor will be sitting in the audience. Go to center stage. If it is a room, she will be behind a table or next to a camera. Stand about six feet in front of her or go to the mark if there is one.

If you are performing a monologue in a theater situation, some people believe that you should introduce yourself and announce the monologues you are going to perform. Other people believe that you should simply say hi and start. You decide what you feel most comfortable doing. You may be told before the audition what the auditor wants. The auditor may ask you what you are going to perform.

If you are performing a monologue in a theater or a room, do not deliver it to the auditor. This makes her nervous. She does not want to be in the scene with you and have to respond. She wants to observe you. Pick a spot in the theater or room and deliver the monologue to that spot. Pick a spot close to the auditor so she can see your face. Talking to an imaginary person or people is awkward. Practice doing it. This is one of the main reasons you should not be bringing an unpolished monologue to an audition. You are already nervous because of the nature of the situation. You are talking to an imaginary person, which for most of us is abnormal. And you are performing. If you add the challenge of getting into character and remembering the lines, you are making things difficult for yourself. An actor who has been auditioning for twenty years can pull this off. If you are new to auditioning, rehearse your monologue.

On rare occasions, the auditor will say it's OK to deliver the monologue to her. If she says it is OK, and that's what you want, then talk directly to her. Try to elicit a response from her. It does get tricky if she is stone-faced. You don't know whether she is uninterested or unimpressed or the kind of person who shows little emotion. She could love what you're doing. If you're not getting the response you want, use it. Stay in character and try to get her to respond. Let her response or lack of response affect you, the character. Do not ask if you can say the monologue to her. If she doesn't bring it up, the answer is probably "no." If you do ask and she says "no," it is an awkward situation.

Don't touch the auditor. Don't offer to shake hands with the auditor. Don't get near the auditor. Don't scare the auditor. Even if you have an impulse, as your character, to playfully tousle the auditor's hair, don't do it.

When you enter the room, you are already in character. You are ready to start. Don't lower your head or turn around and take a moment to get into character. Start the monologue.

If you are doing a scene, you may have a reader. A reader is someone who either works for the auditor or is volunteering for the auditor. She is generally sitting down near the auditor. She might be friendly and a wonderful actress. She might be in a bad mood and a terrible actress. Stay in character and use whatever the reader gives you. The auditor might be the only person in the room with you and she might read with you.

SLATING

If you are auditioning on camera, sometimes you will be asked to slate. Slating is when you look straight into the camera and say your name. You may be asked you say your age if you are under eighteen years old. The producers of a film need to know if you are under eighteen. There are labor and union rules they have to adhere to even if you are not part of a union. You may be asked to say something about yourself. You may be asked a specific question like, "What do you like to do in your spare time?" Have at least five things, unrelated to acting, to talk about with an auditor. If you are asked a question, the auditor is trying to get a sense of your personality. She is just trying to get a sense of who you are as a person. Sometimes you will be asked to do a tail slate. This is when you slate at the end of the audition. Sometimes you won't be asked to slate.

One of the only times you ever look into the lens of the camera is when you slate. The only other time is when it is written in the script that your character looks into the lens or the director asks you to look into the lens. Otherwise, if you look into the lens while in character, it is called "spiking the camera." It ruins the shot and you look like you don't know what you're doing. This drives directors and editors crazy. They may not notice when you spike the camera during shooting, but they will notice in the editing room. An auditor, director or producer will watch your audition tape or the dailies (footage shot that day) and notice if you spike the camera.

Most actors have an irresistible urge to look at the camera lens. The camera is intimidating and mysterious and you want to get a better look at it. In everyday life, we are asked to pose for photos or talk to a video camera. We're trained to look at the camera. While acting, this habit must be eliminated. The camera is the audience. You wouldn't look at the audience during a live performance. That would be breaking the fourth wall. It's like saying, "Hi. Am I doing OK? What are you looking at? Why are you looking at me? Enjoying the show?" Don't break the fourth wall. Don't spike the camera.

Practice doing your monologues at home in front of a camera. Pick a scene, break it down and rehearse it in front of a camera. While rehearsing, imagine that the auditor is someone you really respect.

THE FORTY-FIVE-DEGREE RULE AND HOT SPOTS

We want the camera to pick up what we are experiencing. The camera cannot capture what we are doing if we are in profile or if our back is turned to the camera. For the most part, not always, we want to adhere to the forty-five-degree rule. (The forty-five-degree rule is closely related to the concept of cheating out.) For the most part, not always, we want our eyes directed toward the "hot spots." (See diagrams on pages 56 and 57) For an audition, it is wise to adhere to these two principles. While shooting a film, it is wise to adhere to them but not to allow them to become inhibiting. Actors break these rules all time. Some actors don't adhere to them at all. A scene can be played looking down at the floor, with the camera never capturing the actors' eyes. These scenes can be riveting. Experience and experimentation will help you figure out what works for you. The given circumstances, direction and other factors will influence how the scene is played. However, you should feel comfortable in front of the camera with your eyes on a hot spot if that is what is required of you in the scene.

HOLDING THE SCRIPT

You should hold the script up so that you can easily look at the script and the reader (if there is one). You do not want to have the script at your side and look down and up repeatedly. Bouncing your head up and down is distracting. You want your eyes visible as much as possible. If the auditor is standing on the right side of the camera (your right), have the script in your right hand. If the auditor is standing on the left side of the camera (your left), have the script in your left hand.

If you know some or all of the lines, you can have the script down at your side. The first audition is not a memorization test. Unless you are performing one or more monologues, you do not need to memorize the material.

You are expected to have the sides or script in your hands. Auditors get nervous if you walk in and don't have the sides with you. If it is a few lines, that's different. Most likely, you can memorize a few lines and the auditors trust that you can pull it off. If it is a page or more of dialogue, the auditors want you to have the sides in your hands and ready to reference in case you drop a line or lose your place. There isn't enough time to start over and they don't have time for apologies. There is nothing wrong with bumbling a line or forgetting a line in a first audition. Stay in character no matter what happens. The auditors are looking at you and determining if you are right for the character. At this point in the process, they are not evaluating your memorization skills.

Take a look at the sample sides and the following diagrams.

Marvin

INT. MARVIN'S KITCHEN - LATER

Marvin enters the kitchen. Mom is reading a book.

Start →

MARVIN
Thank you for making chicken and mashed potatoes for dinner. That's my favorite.

MOM
You're welcome. I hope you feel better.

MARVIN
You're a good mom. The best.

MOM
Thanks.

MARVIN
I do feel better. You were right. It will take some time, but it's not the end of the world. I'll have a piece of pizza and let time heel my wounds.

MOM
No. I don't want you to have pizza. We're eating in a little bit.

MARVIN
Please. Pizza is my favorite thing in the world and it would help.

MOM
That's your sister's pizza. I told her I would save the leftovers.

MARVIN
Great. Nothing ever works out for me.

MOM
Stop → Don't be dramatic.

MARVIN
I have nothing. All I have is this certificate of participation from the dance competition. I'll hang it next to my participation award from soccer.

MOM
Marvin, find something to read or watch a movie.

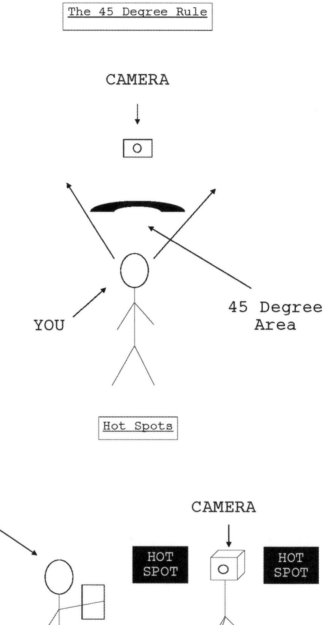

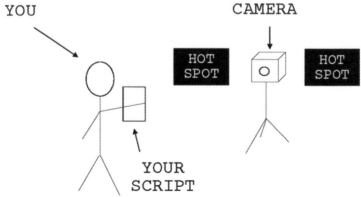

Holding the Script

AUDITOR

CAMERA

YOU

YOUR
SCRIPT

YOUR
MARK

ASK QUESTIONS

If you've had time with the audition material, then you should be able to pronounce every word correctly. You should understand every reference that is made. If something is unclear to you with regard to your character, situation or relationship, ask questions. Auditors are usually very happy to help clarify things for you. They want you to succeed. Very often, an auditor may ask if you have any questions. In a cold read, the auditor anticipates your having questions.

READING WITH OTHER ACTORS

In some cases, you will read with another actor or actors in front of the auditor. It's a rough and unrehearsed performance. It feels awkward and uncomfortable. Focus on listening to the person who is speaking and responding. Your main goal is to make a connection with the other character or characters.

THE AUDITION MINDSET

An audition is more than an evaluation of how you present yourself and how prepared you are. The other factors that affect your getting cast are out of your control.

You are being evaluated on many things. These are some of them:

1. Do you look the part? Are they looking for someone who is 5'3" with auburn hair and hazel eyes? Long or short hair may be a determining factor. They may ask, "Are you willing to cut your hair?" or "Are you willing to grow your hair?" Sometimes, despite having a very specific type that they are looking for, they may discover that the part does not need to be played by someone with the physical attributes they originally envisioned. They realize that an actor with different physical attributes can play the part. Sometimes, auditors don't know what they're looking for and are open with regard to type. The worst example of the situation being out of your control is when you don't get cast because you look like someone the auditor doesn't like. If you look like the kid who used to bully the auditor at school, your chances of being cast are not good.

2. How do you look compared to the other people being considered for the other parts in the production? It is very unlikely that you and someone with very similar physical attributes will be cast as best friends. The audience has a hard time differentiating between two people who look similar.

3. Are you right for the part? If the character is a high-energy person and you are laid back, then you probably won't get that part.

4. Are you talented? You are definitely being evaluated on your talent. This is the most difficult aspect of an audition. If you

don't get the part, it is easy to get down on yourself and question your talent. It can seem like a personal assault. You must keep in mind that judging talent is subjective. Some people will like your work. Some people won't like your work. As discussed earlier in this book, you are in control of how you feel about your work. If you aren't in control, acting can be a very stressful, disappointing and exhausting roller-coaster ride.

THE CALLBACK

You may be cast after a first audition, or you may be called back one or more times. In a callback, you may be paired with other actors and given direction. You may be told to do exactly what you did in the first audition. A callback is an opportunity for the auditors to take another look at you. You should have your lines memorized for a callback. You may be asked to add, change or remove lines.

Auditors are looking to see how you handle a high-pressure situation. While an audition and a performance are different in many ways, they share one common element: both are high-pressure situations. Whether you are in a school play or on Broadway, there are people waiting for the show to start and then watching your performance. If you are filming, people are watching and there is the extra pressure of knowing that what you are doing is being recorded and archived forever. Yes, you are in control of how you feel about your performance. But nothing can get your heart beating and your stomach fluttering quite like knowing that people are about to watch you perform. The feeling is inescapable. At its worst, it is stage fright and you become debilitated. At its best, it is a rush of adrenaline that some-how heightens your level of concentration. Auditors want to know that you will not crack under pressure and that you have nerves of steel.

THE AUDITOR IS ROOTING FOR YOU

The auditor wants you to do well. She is rooting for you. If the auditor has brought you in, then she has confidence that you may be right for the part. If you do well and get cast, the auditor has succeeded. Auditors take great pride in finding the right actor for every role. The best auditors consider casting an art. If she does not do a good job, she is out of work. The old saying in show business is, "Casting is everything." Whether it is a play at school or a big-budget Hollywood film, the auditor wants you to walk in and nail it. An auditor has a problem; she has not found the right actor for the role. You are the solution to her problem.

THE AUDITOR AND YOU

Your primary goal is developing your relationship with the auditor. You may not be right for the current project, but you may be right for her upcoming project or her friend's project. Your reputation and word of mouth will open doors.

TYPECASTING

Some actors are scared of being typecast. This means that they don't want to get known as an actor who can only play a certain type of character. For example, they've played the gregarious, loudmouthed and angry character, and they want to try other types.

When you're first starting out as an actor, it is best to figure out what parts are right for you. Those are the parts that you connect with and that you will feel comfortable doing. Those are the parts that you will most likely get. Once you have gotten experience doing those roles, then you can start to broaden your range. Getting cast at all is challenging. The competition is fierce. Trying to get cast for a part for which you are not right makes things very difficult.

ACTING SCHOOLS, CLASSES AND THEATERS

Auditioning for an acting school, class or theater is slightly different from auditioning for a specific project. Different institutions have different criteria for what they believe an actor should possess in order to fit into their program or group.

For a school that provides acting training, in addition to your professionalism, you are being evaluated on your potential. "Does this person have the passion, work ethic and raw talent to be a valuable member of our community?" Most of the time, auditors have enough experience to make this determination quickly.

A theater that is looking to add members to their repertory group is focused on your type. If they need someone to play the female character roles in their upcoming series of plays and you fit that type, then your chances are good.

FINAL THOUGHTS ON AUDITIONING

Prepare, stay relaxed and concentrate.

REJECTION, TALENT AND CONFIDENCE

Rejection and acting go hand in hand. You will not get every part you want. Someone usually says something negative about your performance. Someone usually gives you advice on how your performance could be better.

It is often said that an actor needs thick skin. That may be true. However, if you are not dependent on praise or criticism, then you don't need thick skin. Having thick skin means that you are unaffected by others or situations. It requires you to close yourself off and be insensitive. Sensitivity is one of the things that distinguishes an actor. Actually, the degree of sensitivity an individual possesses reflects his or her level of talent. Our job, as actors, is to express what a character is experiencing. Our craft demands that we be expressive. We cannot be expressive unless we are sensitive. We cannot block out the world, ignore our emotions and at the same time be expressive. Being thick-skinned is counterproductive and borderline schizophrenic. Being thick-skinned is exhausting and unhealthy.

Rejection and disappointment are a part of life that everybody experiences. An actor experiences rejection and disappointment regularly. A confident actor believes in his talent. He accepts negativity and then disregards it. He then focuses on his next artistic endeavor. "You didn't like my performance? I didn't get the part? Well, I liked my performance. I think I was right for that part. That's too bad. Now I'll focus on something that I find interesting."

An actor must be confident or his artistic spirit will not survive.

PRODUCING YOUR OWN WORK

Pursuing acting opportunities requires time and effort. Part of being a working, paid or professional actor is navigating the business. A successful professional actor is usually a good businessman. If you are not interested in being a professional actor, or acting is a hobby, you still have to spend time and energy finding projects.

Whatever your situation, there are only so many projects out there. There are only so many parts that are right for you. There will be dry spells. You must fulfill your creative needs.

Actors are at the mercy of other people when it comes to getting cast. Writing and performing your own material is one solution to fulfilling your creative needs in between projects or when you are tired of depending on other people for roles. It is empowering to produce your own play or film. Work with like-minded people in a group or work alone. You may find that writing is not your thing. If you are working with a group, you may discover that you enjoy set design, costume design or some other aspect of production.

When working with a group, the group's chances of survival are better if one person is in charge. There should be one person making the final decisions about everything. Personality conflicts arise. Artistic opinions differ. Even something as simple as scheduling rehearsals can be a major challenge. One person should be at the head and either control all aspects of the decision-making process or delegate wisely.

CHAPTER 10

THE BUSINESS OF ACTING

This section lays out basic information about the acting business. This is information you need to know if you want to seek work in the professional world. If you are under the age of eighteen, you will need assistance from a parent or guardian in order to execute certain aspects of the business. This section is as much for a parent or guardian of a young actor as it is for an actor.

If you are under eighteen and are interested in seeking work as a professional, you must understand that you are a kid or young adult in an adult world. You must behave like a responsible and mature adult or you won't be taken seriously.

The information outlined here will apply differently based on the area of the United States in which you live. Things work a little differently in New York than they do in Los Angeles, Chicago or any other part of the country. The acting business has changed in different ways over the years and will continue to change. Be sure to get the most up-to-date information.

My goal here is to explain the basics and eliminate some of the mystery of how the business works. You may decide that you do not want to get involved in the business. If you decide that you must get involved, there are numerous books, classes, web videos and other resources that delve deeply into every aspect of the business.

If you decide to pursue work as a professional or to help your child pursue work, you must realize that it takes as much business sense and skill to start a business as an actor as it does to start any other kind of business.

BEING A PROFESSIONAL ACTOR

In the traditional sense, a professional or working actor is:

1. A union member

2. Someone who devotes a significant amount of time to pursuing paying acting jobs

3. Someone who earns all or most of his income working as an actor

If you are an adult and you want to be a professional actor, you have to be confident that there is nothing else in the world that will make you happy besides acting.

If you are under eighteen, then you have to love acting and be comfortable sacrificing some or all of your time at school, with friends, with family and exploring other interests.

The day-to-day life of an adult actor is something like this:

1. He works a side or survival job. Side or survival work includes but is not limited to temporary work, retail work or work as an assistant in an office. This is essentially any job that is flexible. He is able to switch his schedule in order to go to an audition or take time off for an acting job.

2. He takes acting classes.

3. He goes on auditions. He may have five auditions in a week. He may have five auditions in a month. Most auditions are on weekdays between 9:00 a.m. and 6:00 p.m. Sometimes there are auditions and callbacks on Saturdays and Sundays.

4. He books acting jobs regularly.

It could take three years until he earns enough money to drop his side or survival job and work only as an actor. It could be twenty years. It could never happen.

The day-to-day life of an actor under the age of eighteen is something like this:

1. He gets an audition and has to leave school early that day and miss a test.

2. He goes to a family function and gets a call from his agent, who says that he has an audition in an hour.

3. He books a job in another city or state and has to leave town for three weeks.

4. He takes acting classes after school or on the weekends.

If you are under the age of eighteen, ask yourself:

1. Do I love acting?

2. Am I willing to commit to acting 100 percent?

3. Do I have enough training and experience to know what to do and how to behave in a professional setting?

AGENTS

An agent is someone who sets up auditions for you. Agencies come in all sizes and can function in many different ways.

Smaller agencies, sometimes referred to as boutique agencies, may have a few agents who represent actors "across the board." This means that one or more agents will submit you for theater work, film work, commercials, print and voice-overs. Some agencies deal with comedians, hosts for live events and pretty much any kind of work that pays.

Mid-sized and larger agencies might be divided into specific departments. For example, an agency will have one or more agents dealing only with film work.

It is an agent's job to submit you for projects. It is not an agent's job to get you work. The agent sets up the audition. It's up to you to book the job.

If you book the job, the agent or agency takes 10 percent of whatever you make.

MANAGERS

Agents handle your career on a day-to-day basis. A manager takes a special interest in you and your career. She will think about your career in the long term and help you devise a game plan. In some cases, she is allowed to submit you for union work.

A manager will take 10 to 15 percent of whatever you make. This is in addition to the 10 percent you will pay if you are working with an agent.

Some people believe that actors do not need managers. Some people think managers are helpful. A solid argument can be made both for and against working with a manager. Really, it comes down to where you are in your career, the connections the manager has, the reputation the manager has and what you feel you need. It's a source of constant discussion and debate. In the end, you have to figure out what is best for you and your career.

You can have conversations with a manager that go something like this:

> "I just booked a part in a touring production. It's a great credit and good money, but I'll be on the road for a significant amount of time. It will affect my personal life in a huge way. I may miss bigger opportunities. But the tour may lead to something bigger. What do you think?"

An agent, on the other hand, may or may not be interested in having this type of conversation. Some agents believe that if they worked to get you the audition for the touring production and you booked it, you'd better take it. They either want the money or don't want to make the uncomfortable call to the casting director to tell her you declined. That being said, a manager might feel the same way.

Under no circumstances should you ever pay an agent or manager unless you have booked a job and been paid. Anyone who asks for money up front and promises to get you auditions is a fraud.

CASTING DIRECTORS

A casting director is responsible for casting a project. She is hired by a producer, director or advertising agency. Her job is to pick actors to bring into a casting session and then run the casting session. She may voice her opinion about who should be cast, but ultimately it is up to the producer, director or advertising agency.

HOW DO I GET AN AGENT OR MANAGER?

There are many ways to obtain representation. These are some of the ways it is done:

1. You may submit directly to an agent or manager. An agent's or manager's office usually has a section on its website that gives directions on how to submit your headshot and résumé. You will submit either by mail or through e-mail.

   There are many resources, books and websites that also detail this information.

If you are submitting yourself to an agent or manager, you want to include an introductory letter, a headshot and a résumé. Unless the office requests that you send your materials to the submission department, it's best to target one agent or manager and not the whole office.

The same approach described above applies to contacting casting directors. Some actors send letters, headshots and résumés to casting directors in order to introduce themselves with the hope that the casting director will remember them.

Don't ever go to an agent, manager or casting director's office unless you have been invited or you have seen in writing that it is OK to stop by.

2. There are schools where you can meet with agents, managers, casting directors, directors and other people in the business. You pay for the class, seminar or meeting. You do a monologue, a scene or a song. You may meet with the agent, manager or casting director one on one. If things go well, she will contact you to set up a meeting so you can talk more.

   Research and find out what schools have a solid reputation. Attending these types of schools is a good and effective way to meet people in the business. Many actors have made connections this way.

3. A showcase, executed expertly, can work well. A showcase is an evening of scenes organized by a group of actors. You invite industry people to attend the showcase. You hope that they will like your work and call you in for a meeting.

4. A friend may introduce you to her agent. Your uncle may know a manager. You may meet someone on the street who is an agent. It can happen in any imaginable way.

An agent or manager is looking for someone she can sell. She uses your looks or your credits as a selling point. She might make a call to a friend who is a casting director and say, "You have to see this new actor I just signed. He's very talented." Agents and managers are trying to make money. You are the product.

An agent or manager wants someone who is available for auditions any day of the week during business hours (including Saturday and Sunday).

She wants someone who is available for acting jobs at any time of the day and on any day of the week.

When you are first starting out, it is difficult to find representation. If you are new to the business, then you do not have very many credits. Once you have gotten training and have developed as an artist, then it is time to build your résumé. Work with small theater companies and on low-budget films. Meet people. It may take a while, but in time you will build your résumé, make connections and possibly be seen in a play or film. Maybe a low-budget film gets great exposure at film festivals, or a play you are in gets a favorable review. Agents, managers and casting directors want to work with experienced, dedicated, trained and serious actors who are professional.

Some actors quickly find representation and book big or small jobs. Some continue to get regular work. Some don't. Some actors wait years to get representation while acting in non-paying productions and taking classes. Some never obtain representation. There are many paths.

Your chances of having a long and satisfying career are greater if you have training and experience, and if you work hard to develop as an artist.

MEETING WITH AN AGENT OR MANAGER

If you are called in to meet with an agent or manager, there are a number of things to keep in mind:

1. Choose a business-casual outfit. For someone under eighteen, this means something you would wear to a nice restaurant. You should look like your headshot and you should look the way you would look if are going to an audition.

2. Be ready to perform one or more monologues. You may be asked to perform in a small room for one agent. You may be asked to perform in the middle of the office in front of everyone who works at that office. You may be put on tape. Be prepared for anything.

3. The person with whom you are meeting may ask you questions about your experience as an actor. But usually she wants to get to know you as a person. Have at least five things to talk about that have nothing to do with acting or the arts. Ask the agent questions and see if she's interesting.

If information about the agent and the agency is not available online or in a book, then ask questions. Find out how many people she represents. Which casting directors does she know well?

A relationship with an agent or manager is similar to any other close relationship in life. You have to like each other, trust each other and want to spend time with each other. In a meeting, you are trying to determine if the relationship will work. An agent or manager you don't like personally is not a good fit.

4. Be ready to answer questions about your type. The agency wants to know how they can sell you. Are you the funny, talkative, outgoing type? Are you the quiet, sensitive, shy and introverted type? Would you play the president of the student council or the school bully?

   We are all different things in different situations. But we tend to embody one type of disposition in most circumstances. We tend be able to play one type of character better than other types of characters.

   Figuring out your type is difficult. It requires a deep understanding of who you are. In your training, you will figure out the type of character that is best for you. If you are under the age of fifteen or so, you may or may not be asked your type.

   You should be able to articulate your type accurately, confidently and quickly.

   An agent loves an actor who knows his type. It makes her job easier and she is confident that she is working with someone who understands this fundamental aspect of the business.

5. You may be asked what actors, films and plays you like. You may be asked what well-known actor you are similar to and the roles he has played that are right for you.

   Some agents, managers and casting directors are fun, funny, trustworthy, interesting people who are passionate about their job and the arts. Some are not.

FREELANCING AND SIGNING

If things go well, the agent or manager will ask you either to freelance or to sign with her.

If you freelance, then no contracts are involved. The agent or manager will submit you for projects. In time, if things go well, you may be asked to sign with her. Until you sign a contract, you can work with other agents or managers.

If you sign with an agent, you cannot work with another agent. The contract will specify the area of the business in which the agent is representing you and other pertinent legal details of the arrangement. For example, if you sign with an agent who will represent you for film work, you cannot be submitted for film work by another agent.

Some of the things you should know are:

1. An agent can represent you "across the board."

2. You can have one agent represent you for theater work and a different agent from a different agency represent you for commercial work. It can work many different ways.

3. You can only have one manager.

4. You can have a manager and work with one or more agents.

THE CASTING PROCESS

This is a simple description of the casting process from beginning to end:

1. A producer, director or advertising agency has a project. We'll refer to this person from now on as the producer.

2. The producer hires a casting director. Some production companies have an in-house casting director.

3. The casting director makes a list of all the characters, writes a character description for each character and creates a breakdown (see the example of a breakdown used earlier in this book).

4. The casting director submits the breakdown to a company called Breakdown Services.

5. Breakdown Services sends out the breakdown electronically to all agents and managers who subscribe to their services.

6. Agents and managers submit actors they feel are right for the role.

7. The casting director picks the actors she wants to see.

8. The agent contacts you about your audition day and time.

9. You either confirm or decline based upon whether you can attend the audition and are available for the production dates.

    Do not go to an audition if you know you cannot accept the job due to a conflict.

10. You will be notified by your agent or manager if you book the job or get a callback. You will not be notified if you do not get the job.

    You may be notified if something went terribly wrong in the audition. For example, if the casting director feels that you were unprepared and you are always unprepared, then she might call your agent. Your agent will call you to remedy this problem.

A casting director can call you in directly. As mentioned earlier, some actors send letters of introduction, headshots and résumés to casting directors with the hope of being called in.

Do not call a casting director unless she has asked you to call her. Do not stop by a casting director's office unless she has invited you to stop by.

MAY I SUBMIT MYSELF?

You have to be a licensed agent in order to subscribe to Breakdown Services. You have to be a manger who meets specific criteria in order to subscribe.

Some actors find ways to get breakdowns and auditions without an agent or manager. This is risky. In 2011, an actor in Los Angeles who had been illegally selling breakdowns to other actors was sentenced to twenty days in jail and Breakdown Services was awarded 1.3 million dollars in damages.

You can, legally, find out that a casting director is casting a project. Unless you know that you are right for a specific role, it is not worth it to submit yourself. A blind submission is usually a waste of time, yet people have gotten called in for auditions after blindly submitting.

HEADSHOTS

A good headshot:

1. Looks like you
2. Shows your personality
3. Has good lighting
4. Is a close-up shot

HEADSHOT TIPS

1. Generally, a shot with you smiling is used when you are submitted for commercial work. A shot with you looking more serious is used for theater and film submissions.

2. It can be shot in a studio or at an exterior location. It doesn't matter where you do it.

3. You should wear a solid-color top.

4. Don't wear white.

5. Don't wear anything with logos or patterns. You want the photo to draw attention to your face and your eyes.

6. Don't wear distracting jewelry.

7. Don't show a lot of skin.

It is very important that you look the same way in person as you do in your headshot. Don't do your hair differently or wear extra makeup for your photo session.

Someone you know can take your headshot for free or you can pay a professional photographer. Whomever you choose, your photographer should know what an actor's headshot looks like versus a school portrait, a snapshot or a photo intended to make an artistic statement. If you plan to hire a photographer, meet with her before your photo session. If you do not like the photographer's personality, your photos will not be good.

An agent or manager can give you a list of recommended photographers. If an agent or manager instructs you to go to a specific photographer, it is a scam.

The photo itself should be an 8 x 10 print. You should have it printed by a professional printer. If you own or have access to a professional-grade printer, that will work. In that case, 8 x 10 paper or 8½ x 11 paper will work. Your name should be on your headshot.

You should have at least one copy of your headshot and résumé with you when you go to an audition. Most of the time, it is not needed, because everything is done digitally, but you should have it just in case.

You should have copies of your headshot and résumé with you whenever you are meeting somebody in the business or there is a possibility of meeting someone in the business.

Some actors have a headshot and résumé with them at all times.

RÉSUMÉ

On the following page, there is a sample résumé.

Some people arrange the height and weight information differently or put contact information on the top left. For the most part, the sample résumé is the standard for how a résumé should be formatted.

YOUR NAME

Height: 5'3"	Hair: Brown	
Weight: 145	Eyes: Brown	Contact: Your Phone Number

FILM

NAME OF FILM	Role	Director or Production Company
NAME OF FILM	Role	Director or Production Company
NAME OF FILM	Role	Director or Production Company

THEATRE

NAME OF PLAY	Role	Director or Name of Theater
NAME OF PLAY	Role	Director or Name of Theater
NAME OF PLAY	Role	Director or Name of Theater

COMMERCIAL CONFLICTS AVAILABLE UPON REQUEST

TRAINING & EDUCATION

NAME OF SCHOOL, Location
  • Teacher Name (Acting)
  • Teacher Name (On Camera Class)
  • Teacher Name (Stage Combat)
NAME OF SCHOOL, Location
NAME OF SCHOOL, Location

SPECIAL AND RELATED SKILLS

All sports (excellent basketball player)
Singing (baritone)
Excellent ballroom dancer
LIST ANYTHING THAT IS INTERESTING!

RÉSUMÉ TIPS

1. If you are auditioning for a play, list your theater credits first.

2. If you are auditioning for a film, list your film credits first.

3. Do not put your age on your résumé.

4. Make sure your agent or manager's contact information is on your résumé.

5. If you don't have an agent or manager, put your phone number on the résumé.

6. If you don't have very many credits, you can include "Representative Roles." These are characters that you have worked on in class.

7. If you are very young, then training and special skills will help you stand out.

8. It's OK to put school plays on your résumé.

9. In most cities, you do not list the commercials in which you have appeared.

10. Use white paper or print the résumé directly on the back of your headshot. If you print it on paper, staple the résumé to the back of your headshot. Trim your résumé so that it is the same height and width as your headshot. There should be a staple on all four corners. Have your headshot and résumé stapled before you go to a meeting or audition.

11. Do not get fancy with your résumé by using colored paper or glitter. Keep it simple and easy to read.

12. Do not put any lies on your résumé.

NON-UNION VS. UNION

In the United States, the union for film, TV and radio is Screen Actors Guild–American Federation of Television and Radio Artists (SAG/AFTRA). In the United States, the union for theater is Actors' Equity Association (Equity). The websites for both unions will give answers to most questions you may have. If one of these websites does not answer your question, call the union.

Here is the basic information you need to know:

1. Non-union productions are unregulated and operate according to their own rules. Most non-union productions adhere to the basic SAG/AFTRA and Equity rules out of respect for actors. Of course, there are exceptions. You should thoroughly research any person or company producing non-union plays or films.

2. Agents, managers and casting directors will work with non-union productions.

3. Non-union work is great for actors just starting out. Usually, these productions are helmed by students, beginners or independent producers.

4. When you are just starting out or are in the early stages of your career, there are more opportunities in the non-union world. You can get these auditions or jobs on your own without the assistance of an agent or manager.

5. You can audition for a union job even if you are not a member of the union.

6. If you book a union job and you are not a member of a union, you have the option to join the union.

7. Once you join the union, you are not allowed to work on non-union productions unless the production company or individual producer files the proper paperwork with SAG/AFTRA or Equity. SAG/AFTRA and Equity have special contracts and agreements for these situations.

The benefit of joining one or both of the unions has to be evaluated on an individual basis.

EXTRA WORK

Extra work, sometimes called background work, is a great way learn how a set is run. If you are lucky, you may be upgraded to a speaking role. Doing extra work is a respectable way to obtain knowledge about filmmaking. However, in the professional world, extra work is not considered acting work and it should not be put on your resume.

FINAL NOTES ON THE BUSINESS

If you book a job, it is expected that you will know what you are doing once the production starts. Mistakes made by a ten-year-old are forgiven more easily than those made by a fifteen-year-old. If a twenty-two-year-old is unprepared in any way, he may have just ruined his career or significantly damaged his reputation.

A trained and experienced actor is given more respect than an untrained actor. If I am going to court, I am going to want an educated and experienced lawyer to represent me. If I need surgery, I am going to want an educated and experienced surgeon. If I have secured enough money to produce a film or play, I am going to hire actors who are trained and experienced. It requires the same dedication and hard work to become a great actor as it does to become an Olympic athlete or concert pianist.

The business of acting takes a significant amount of time, research, effort, energy and money.

FINAL NOTES ON ACTING

Acting is never easy. It is a challenging and rewarding craft that takes years of dedication, hard work and practice. The best actors take acting seriously and spend a lifetime striving to develop as artists.

If you are just starting out, you may not know how much time and effort you want to commit to acting. Some people devote their lives to this artistic process. Some people enjoy acting as an extracurricular activity while pursuing other interests.

Whatever your goal is, while studying acting, you can learn valuable information about life, the human condition and yourself. Acting is a powerful and enjoyable form of self-expression.

CHAPTER 11

WRITING AND WRITING EXERCISES

If you enjoy acting as a form of expression, you might get pleasure from writing. Take what you have learned about creating a character and use this knowledge while executing the following writing exercises.

Before you get started on the exercises, here is some helpful information about the art of storytelling.

WHAT MAKES A STORY?

A story is about somebody who wants something. By the end of the story, he either gets what he wants or he does not. Generally, a story has a beginning, middle and end.

STRUCTURE

In the beginning of the story, a character is going about his normal life.

An incident happens that upsets the character's normal life and propels him into action. This incident, sometimes called the "inciting incident," thrusts the character into fighting for something that he wants. It could be that the character is fighting against something he does not want.

The story progresses as the character struggles to get what he wants. He has small and large successes and failures. Forces of antagonism—internal, interpersonal and external—prevent him from achieving his goal. The story can progress in one or more ways:

1. The character takes action.

2. Another character takes action.

3. The character reveals information.

4. Another character reveals information.

The character reaches a point where action is taken or information is revealed that either does or does not allow him to get what he wants. This is the climax.

Note: A story can progress because characters choose not to take action. A story can move forward because information is withheld.

The story is then resolved. The character has gone on a journey and is now different, in some way, than he was when the story started. Sometimes the character does not undergo any kind of change.

Some or all of the elements described above may appear in your story. Generally, it is important to show the audience the inciting incident and the climax.

This is a very elementary explanation of what builds a compelling and interesting story. Storytelling technique and theory is a whole area of study that rests outside the world of acting. However, many actors find great pleasure in writing and many writers are drawn to acting. Creative people often like to dabble in multiple art forms.

STORY EXAMPLE

Let's look at the story we began working with when we practiced script analysis in Chapter 8.

Normal Life: Marvin spends most of his time playing video games.

Inciting Incident: Marvin's friend Ike signs Marvin up for a dance competition. The winner of the competition gets to be part of a supergroup.

Progression: Marvin practices. He goes to a party and everyone cheers him on as he shows off his moves. Ike informs Marvin that in order to win the competition, Marvin has to invent and perform an original dance move. Marvin works hard to invent an original dance move. Marvin suffers from heat exhaustion and is bedridden. The day of the dance competition, Marvin is still sick.

Climax: The dance competition is under way. Marvin drags himself out of bed, gets to the dance competition and performs his routine with great success. While the judges are tabulating their scores,

Marvin sees Ike give a judge a bribe. Later, Ike is announced as the winner of the competition.

Resolution: Marvin teaches dance and earns money to help save for his college education.

This may be a great idea for a story. Maybe it needs some fine-tuning. Or, you may realize that your time is better spent developing a different story. Whatever the case, you want to make sure that, if you spend time working on a story,

1. It is interesting to you and will keep your interest from the beginning to the end of the writing process.

2. The main idea behind the story is something that you believe. The main idea behind the story above is something along the lines of "Win or lose, you can gain something from working hard." Maybe that's what the story is about. You won't really know until you spend more time developing the story. You may or may not know the main idea, or theme, of the story until you are well into the writing process. However, the main thrust behind a story should be rooted in your belief system. You may believe that hard work is worthwhile and that working hard on something is an opportunity to grow no matter what kind of success you achieve. You may not be sure this story about Marvin and the dance competition is the way you want to express your belief. In this case, you need to let some time pass and think about it. In some cases, you will know right away if a story is going to work.

These principles and ideas can be applied to a one-page scene or a feature-length film.

PLAYS AND FILMS

Plays and films can be set in one location or have multiple locations. There can be one character or hundreds of characters.

A play, generally, uses dialogue to explore the thoughts, feelings and beliefs of a character. A play is dialogue-driven.

A film shows the audience what a character thinks, feels and believes through a character's action. When you write a screenplay, you are describing what the audience is seeing. "Show, don't tell" is the maxim often used in the screenwriting world.

FORMAT

There is a specific format for plays, screenplays, teleplays, commercials and every other kind of creative writing.

For example, the script breakdown sample on page 28 is in play format. The sides sample on page 59 is in screenplay format.

WHERE DO I GET AN IDEA FOR A STORY?

Ideas can come from anywhere.

You can:

1. Use an experience, relationship or anything from your life to spark an idea for a story.

2. Get an idea from somebody else's experience.

3. Read something that sparks an idea.

4. Use your imagination.

5. Have a burst of inspiration.

WORKSHEET AND EXERCISES

The "Idea-Generating Exercises" are designed to spark ideas for stories. I have imposed guidelines. With limitation comes freedom.

The "Story Worksheet" is designed to help you plan out the major details of a story. You do not have to start with the first question and work your way through it. You can start anywhere you want and jump around. You may write down an idea and then get a better idea because of a choice you made for a different story element. Many writers start with the ending and work backward.

WRITING EXERCISES

Idea-Generating Exercise #1

Guidelines

- Pick any sentence below and use it as a catalyst.
- Your story cannot have dialogue.

- Pick a genre for your story. Some examples are slapstick comedy, horror and western.
- The story must be no longer than one minute. It can be as short as you want it to be.
- The story must be staged in the room or space where you are right now.
- Do not use bathroom humor or inappropriate subject matter.

Sentences

"I lost my mind thinking about it."

"I left my bag downstairs."

"This isn't what I wanted in life."

"I couldn't decide what to wear this morning."

"Watch this. I've never done it before."

"There's something very odd happening."

"Why me? Why does this always happen to me?"

"When do you think this is going to change?"

"This hurts. This also hurts. Does this hurt?"

"My parents would be ashamed of me right now."

"Some people will never understand."

"She's the best. I wish I could be like her."

"What a waste."

"I'm uncomfortable. Very uncomfortable."

"I knew this was a mistake."

"Leftovers taste better than the original."

"This is where I had a meltdown."

Idea-Generating Exercise #2

Guidelines

- Pick any sentence below and use it as a catalyst.
- Your story can have a maximum of six lines of dialogue.
- You must use one or more of the lines below in your story.

- Pick a genre for your story. Some examples are slapstick comedy, horror and western.

- The story must be no longer than three minutes long. It can be as short as you want it to be.

- The story must be staged in the room or space where you are right now.

- Do not use bathroom humor, inappropriate language or inappropriate subject matter.

Sentences

"Over there, it's over there."

"This is the last time I'm doing this."

"Everything must come to an end."

"This is so dumb."

"My brain hurts thinking about it."

"I'll never do that again."

"I made this."

"This doesn't work. It never has."

"It feels weird in here."

"It's too bad."

"What a shame."

"Keep working on it. You'll get it."

"Now you're thinking."

"I've been waiting a long time for this."

"Nothing excites me more."

"Put it back."

"This doesn't feel right."

Idea-Generating Exercise #3

Guidelines

- Pick the most embarrassing thing that has ever happened to you and use that as a catalyst for your story. You do not have to expose your embarrassing moment. Mask the embarrassing moment by changing the details of the event.

- Your story can have as much dialogue as you want.
- Pick a genre for your story. Some examples are slapstick comedy, horror and western.
- The story can be as long or as short as you want.
- The story can have as many locations as you want.
- Do not use bathroom humor, inappropriate language or inappropriate subject matter.

STORY WORKSHEET

Story Structure

Beginning

- Your character is going about her daily life.
- Maybe something is missing in her life. Maybe she is aware of this. Maybe she is not aware of this.
- Describe what her life is like.

Inciting incident

- Something happens at the top of the story that upsets her world and propels her into action. She now wants something.
- Describe this incident. Describe what she wants.

Progression

- She works to get what she wants. She has small and big successes and failures.

Describe

- One big success
- One small failure
- One big failure

Climax

- She reaches a point where she or someone else takes action. Or she or someone else reveals information. She either gets what she wants or does not.

- Describe the action your character or another character takes or the information your character or another character reveals.

Resolution

- We see the character after she gets or does not get what she wanted.
- Describe what your character's life is like.

Additional Questions

1. What is your character's overall objective?
2. What obstacles does she encounter in the pursuit of what she wants?
3. Does she get what she wants?
4. By the end of the story, how has her life changed?

CHAPTER 12

SHORT MONOLOGUES

The following monologues are open with regard to gender. Interpretation is open with regard to the person to whom the character is speaking, where the character is and all other relevant choices that need to be made by the actor.

I would be comforted by the fact that I know someday he'll be gone, but I'm positive that some other jerk will take his place.

I don't know if people who always have a smile on their face are happy or dumb. They don't know that life is very difficult or they just haven't been told.

Some of our most creative people and best leaders are self-centered egoists who have great compassion for society but little respect for the people closest to them. I am one of those people.

I don't talk to most of my old friends. I've changed. They've changed or they've moved away. I miss the friendships I had, but I know that the friendship I would have with those people now would be disappointing. Especially with the people who moved away.

I am a scientist. I can measure things and think critically. Therefore I can understand the world. The physical part of it. Not people necessarily. I live in my head. Not in my body. That's why I have so many health problems. I don't have the capacity to take care of my body. Just my brain.

I have made a decision about how I feel about the death penalty. I think that if someone has taken someone else's life, then they should suffer the same fate. Get rid of them. They don't deserve to live. They shouldn't take up space in our prisons. On the other hand they should have to suffer in prison and have to live with what they did. Unless they die and there actually is a hell. I don't know. I guess I haven't made up my mind.

My grandfather is in his seventies. He has Alzheimer's and is in bad shape. Last week, he didn't know me. He falls a lot and has to go to the hospital. He was diagnosed about ten years ago. My grandmother doesn't know what to do. The saddest part about this is that he has one friend who comes to visit him once a week. All of his other friends have abandoned him. What does that say about the human condition?

People say things, make promises. Perhaps they're sincere but then they forget or realize that they can't fulfill their promises. It's really terrible. My point is . . . I don't think we should see each other anymore.

I couldn't fall asleep last night so I read for about two hours and then I put on a documentary. Not a loud one but one of those boring ones on PBS about the Hoover Dam. I got sucked in because it was actually interesting. I didn't fall asleep until 4 a.m. I don't remember anything about the Hoover Dam.

I checked in the guest and then I asked him if his dog was going to be staying with him. He said yes. I explained that there would be a fifteen-dollar fee.

He asked if I could waive the fee. I said no. You told me that I should never waive the fee. The guest proceeded to raise his voice and use profanity. I remained calm. He then called me a "retard." That's when I threw my pen at him. Right after that, you walked up. So, what's it going to be, Sally? Are you with him or me?

✦

I don't want to hang out with you anymore. You always want something. You want a favor or you want to borrow something or you want advice. It's always something. So let's just make this easy and go our separate ways. Here. Here's the glass you left at my place. I'd like to get my drill back. Can you drop it off this week?

✦

Hey, you look good. You look fit. I was watching you, though. When you do squats, you need to make sure your knees don't come out over your toes. That puts pressure on your back and you'll blow it out like I did a couple years ago. I blew it out so bad I couldn't walk for three months. I'm a personal trainer, so if you ever need personal training you should let me know, because I am a personal trainer.

✦

I am a piano player. Always have been. But, like many people who flee from the things they're good at, I have bigger dreams than being part of some pop band or a symphony. I want to compose my own symphonies or be the front man for a band. Well, I don't have the talent to lead and that will be my downfall. So be it. I'd rather strive for bigger things and fail and end up playing at the mall than not have tried. I'm doomed to be insignificant either way.

✦

I don't think I'm smarter than everyone. I know I'm smarter than everyone and I wish everyone would just shut up and listen. If they did, then we wouldn't have any more problems and we could move forward. But that's not going to happen, and I just ruined my chances of making that happen by saying what I just said.

❖

My grandfather gave me this watch for my birthday. He usually forgets my birthday. This year he remembered and he actually gave me a present. He usually gives me two presents on Christmas. One is for Christmas and one is for my birthday. I've tried to get to know him, but he's very quiet and doesn't open up. This watch means a lot to me. You can have it for fifty dollars.

❖

I understand that you've been through something extreme. You say that words can't express how you're feeling right now. Well, if you can't find the words, then we need to buy you a dictionary and thesaurus so that you have the proper tools to express yourself.

❖

I stole it. I steal things every now and then. Stupid stuff like business card holders off people's desks and photographs on the walls in restaurant bathrooms. But this time I stole someone's cell phone. I couldn't resist. And this time it wasn't for kicks, supposing I had stolen the other stuff for kicks. This time it was because my friend called me a thief. I took revenge by stealing his cell phone.

❖

I can't remember anything. I live in a cut-and-paste, e-mail-a-note-to-myself, remind-me-to-do-this-or-that world. A friend once told me she was losing her memory and then she was diagnosed with brain cancer three weeks later. Then she died. I don't think I have brain cancer, because I've never been able to remember anything. I'm either stupid or brilliant with a twist of absent-mindedness.

❖

Creative people worry about using their best material and having it go unnoticed and wasted. If you're creative, you can always go deeper. If you're not creative, it's probably wise to save your best material.

SUGGESTED READINGS

A Dream of Passion by Lee Strasberg (Plume, 1988)

Accents: A Manual for Actors by Robert Blumenfeld (Limelight Editions, 2004)

Acting: The First Six Lessons by Richard Boleslavsky (Martino Fine Books, 2013)

An Actor Prepares by Constantin Stanislavsky (Routledge, 1989)

Audition by Michael Shurtleff (Bantam, 1980)

Meisner on Acting by Sanford Meisner (Vintage, 1987)

Respect for Acting by Uta Hagen (Wiley, 2008)

The Actor Speaks by Patsy Rodenburg (St. Martin's Griffin, 2002)

The Art of Acting by Stella Adler (Applause Theatre & Cinema Books, 2000)

Thinking Shakespeare by Barry Edelstein (Spark Pub Group, 2007)